CliffsTestPrep®

California Real Estate Salesperson Exam: 5 Practice Tests

CliffsTestPrep®

California Real Estate Salesperson Exam: 5 Practice Tests

by

By John A. Yoegel, Ph.D., DREI

Wiley Publishing, Inc.

About the Author

John Yoegel has been a real estate instructor for over 20 years and holds the Distinguished Real Estate Instructor designation from the Real Estate Educators Association.

Author's Acknowledgments

I want to thank my wife, the lovely Marina, who has made so many of my endeavors, including this book, possible. Thanks also to my agent, Grace Freedson, who, keeps me busy. I want to thank Acquisitions Editor Greg Tubach for getting me started on the right foot; Project Editor Elizabeth Kuball, who made this book considerably clearer for the readers; and Technical Editor Layne Kulwin, who kept me on the straight and narrow with respect to the nuances of California real estate law and practice. I also wish to thank all of the students who through the years have put themselves in my hands. Sometimes I wonder who learned more, them or me.

Publisher's Acknowledgments

Editorial

Acquisitions Editor: Greg Tubach

Project Editor: Elizabeth Kuball

Technical Editor: Layne Kulwin

Production

Proofreader: Jacqui Brownstein

Wiley Publishing, Inc. Composition Services

CliffsTestPrep® California Real Estate Salesperson Exam: 5 Practice Tests

Published by:
Wiley Publishing, Inc.
111 River Street
Hoboken, NJ 07030-5774
www.wiley.com

Copyright © 2006 Wiley, Hoboken, NJ

Published by Wiley, Hoboken, NJ
Published simultaneously in Canada

Library of Congress Cataloging-in-Publication data is available from the publisher upon request.

ISBN-13: 978-0-470-03699-0

ISBN-10: 0-470-03699-0

10 9 8 7 6 5 4 3 2 1

1O/SQ/QX/QW/IN

WILEY

Table of Contents

PART I

INTRODUCTION TO THE CALIFORNIA REAL ESTATE SALESPERSON EXAM

Introduction

Thank you for purchasing CliffsTestPrep *California Real Estate Salesperson Exam: 5 Practice Tests.* With this book, the material you learned in your courses and from your textbooks, and a little hard work, you'll be well prepared to take and pass the California exam and be on your way to a rewarding career in the real estate industry.

The principal purpose of this book is to provide you with practice tests to help you prepare for the state exam, so this introduction is brief. I know you're anxious to get to the practice tests, but I recommend starting by reviewing this introduction, as the material I cover here will help you get the maximum benefit from this book as well as offer some hints to help you do well on the state exam. Before you take your state exam, you may want to review the introduction again, particularly the information on exam taking hints.

I do want to make one note about what this book is *not* and how it should *not* be used. This is neither a textbook nor a reference book; it should be used only as a guide in passing your California real estate exam. To the extent possible, I tried to make the material current and correct in the context in which it is presented. The material is specifically designed around a multiple-choice testing format. As such, vital pieces of information that may change a particular circumstance in real life are often left out. Your ultimate real estate practice should be guided by your courses, textbooks, and ultimately the brokers you work for, in order to maintain compliance with state law.

Although this book will give you practice for the state examination and will help you review the material on the exam, it is no substitute for study. Before tackling these practice tests, you should have a thorough knowledge of the material taught in your pre-licensing courses as well as the textbooks in the courses. You will also want to familiarize yourself with the information at the California Department of Real Estate Web site (www.dre.ca.gov), which has a great deal of information, including additional practice questions. You should also be familiar with the booklet available from the state titled "Reference Book—A Real Estate Guide," which is available online at www.dre.ca.gov/reftoc.htm. Once you feel you have a mastery of the necessary subject matter, begin taking the practice tests in this book.

How This Book Is Organized

The primary material in this book consists of five practice tests, each consisting of 150 multiple-choice questions with an answer key and explanations. The questions are typical of the type of questions that are asked on state real estate examinations. The content of the tests is designed to cover material as outlined at the State of California real estate licensing Web site.

How to Use This Book

I have attempted, in constructing the practice tests, to help you accomplish five goals:

- Practice taking a typical length exam.
- Practice dealing with various types of multiple-choice questions.
- Review important subject matter.
- Self-diagnose the areas in which you need more study.
- Develop your own test taking style.

In the following sections, I give you more information on each of these goals and show you how to accomplish them, remembering that the ultimate goal is to help you pass the state exam.

Practice taking a typical length exam

The California real estate salesperson's license exam consists of 150 multiple-choice questions. You have 3 hours and 15 minutes in which to complete the exam and you must score 70 percent (105 questions correct) in order to pass.

To use the tests in this book for practice, consider the following tips:

- Block out three hours when you won't be interrupted.

- Plan on taking only one practice test at a sitting. These tests are fairly long and your best bet is to approach each one fresh.

- Find a quiet place where you won't be disturbed.

- Prepare your materials, including pencils and a calculator.

- If you want to allow yourself the opportunity to take each practice test more than once, photocopy the answer sheets at the beginning of each test and use your photocopy to record your answers. (If you plan to take each practice test only once, you can freely write in the book.)

- When you take a practice test, make sure you keep track of your time. With exams of this length, tracking your time throughout the exam is important. You need to complete at least 50 questions per hour in order to finish, and that provides no time for review (you'll need to move more quickly through the questions if you want to allow yourself review time).

Practice dealing with various types of multiple-choice questions

I have included several different types of multiple-choice questions in these tests in order to give you practice for the real thing.

The most common type of question is asked in a straightforward manner. This type of question is characterized by a statement, called the *stem,* that calls for picking a single answer from the four choices. The stem is generally constructed as a positive statement or question, such as, "Which of the following activities requires a real estate license?" or "Directions and distances are used in what type of system of legal description?"

The next type of question is asked in the negative and requires the selection of the single answer that does not fit into the group with the remaining answers, such as, "Which of the following activities does not require a real estate license?" The choices will consist of three activities that require a license and one (the correct answer) that does not. These questions are not necessarily more difficult than any other type of question, but after a series of straightforward questions asked in the positive, you need to be alert to the change in language. One way to handle this type of question is to change the stem to a positive statement and check each answer against that statement. In the example I'm using, you would rephrase the stem to read, "You need a real estate license to . . ." and then check each multiple-choice answer against that statement until you get to the one that doesn't need a license.

The third type of question is not really so much a different type of question as a different answer—"all of the above," "none of the above," "both A and B," and so on. There is no trick to answering these questions except knowing the material cold. These answers do, however, provide good study material in that the very nature of the question and answer provides a list of items to remember.

Math questions often create a great deal of anxiety among students and test takers. Once again, there is no substitute for studying and practice. A few cautions, however, are in order when approaching math questions. If you have any math anxiety or special difficulty with math problems, leave them for the end. Be sure to read the question carefully to see what is being asked. Make sure you don't leave out a step like converting from one unit of measure to another (for example, square feet to square yards). Finally, unlike other multiple-choice questions where your first answer is usually the correct one, work the math problem a second time to make sure you didn't copy down the wrong numbers or miss a step. (The incorrect answers in math questions are often answers that you would be likely to get if you made a common mistake, so double-checking your work ensures that you haven't arrived at one of the wrong answers.)

Review important subject matter

I've constructed the questions and provided explanations along with the answers to allow you to go back over the questions and use them as a review. For example, any question where "all of the above" is the correct answer will provide you with a short list of items that you should study. There are a number of variations of different questions on the same topic among the tests. Although no test preparation book can guarantee that any particular topic will be on any specific exam, some subjects are typically covered. I've tried to make sure that these topics are adequately covered in various questions.

Self-diagnose the areas in which you need more study

The way the practice tests in this book have been prepared will allow you to diagnose your weak areas so that you can concentrate your study time accordingly. The questions have been organized in groups according to the subject matter presented by the California Department of Real Estate. You can go to the California Department of Real Estate Web site at www.dre.ca.gov/salesqs.htm to check out the various subjects and percentages of the actual exam allotted to each subject. The following table gives you the question numbers in each of the practice tests relevant to each subject area.

Sections of the Exam	
Section	**Question Numbers on Practice Tests**
Property Ownership and Land Use Controls and Regulations	1–27
Laws of Agency	28–45
Valuation and Market Analysis	46–63
Financing	64–83
Transfer of Property	84–96
Practice of Real Estate and Mandated Disclosures	97–132
Contracts	133–150

After you take each test, in addition to coming up with your total score, you should go back and see what percentage of questions in each area you got right or wrong. By identifying in which subjects you're the strongest and in which subjects you're the weakest, you can concentrate your study efforts on those areas in which you need more work. Be sure to convert the score in each subject to a percentage, because the number of questions in each subject area varies. In other words, if you get 12 Transfer of Property questions correct, and 12 Laws of Agency questions correct, at first glance you might think you know each area equally well. But if you work out the percentages, you actually got 92 percent of the Transfer of Property questions correct (12 correct ÷ 13 total questions) and only 67 percent of the Laws of Agency questions correct (12 correct ÷ 18 total questions).

Ultimately, you should shoot for an overall score of at least 85 to 90 percent for the whole exam and in each individual subject area. This should give you a comfortable margin to pass the state exam. (**Remember:** You need a score of at least 70 percent to pass the exam.)

Develop your own test taking strategy

There are several recommended strategies for taking multiple-choice tests in general and dealing with questions in particular. The five tests in this book will give you a chance to practice different approaches to test taking.

The first approach is to go through the whole exam fairly quickly, answering the questions you know and skipping the ones you don't. Then you go back and spend the remaining time answering those question you skipped. If a question has you stumped, try to eliminate at least one or two answers you know to be wrong. If you can eliminate two answers, even if you have to guess you've increased your odds to a 50-50 chance of guessing correctly. The thing you need to be careful about if you skip questions is keeping track of your place on the answer sheet. You'll have to do all this on scrap paper, because you won't be allowed to write in the test booklet.

The second approach for taking the exam is just to go through each question in order. As I mention earlier, you'll have to keep good track of your time, making sure you don't spend too much time on any one question. It would be a shame to miss several questions that you know the answers to just because you ran out of time.

As for individual question strategies, assuming you have a good grasp of the material, your first instinct on a multiple-choice exam is generally correct. Don't overthink the questions or go back and second-guess yourself. Deal with the material in the question and don't let your imagination create "what if" circumstances that require you to change your answer. There are two exceptions to this advice:

- You should do the math questions twice if you have the time.
- If a later question (say, question 60) provides information that helps you get a better answer to an earlier question (say, question 20), then by all means use that new information and revise your answer.

Above all, read the questions and carefully note what they're asking for. Watch out for the "Which of the following is not . . ." question after a series of positive questions.

Getting Ready for Exam Day

You've studied the necessary material. You've taken each of the practice tests perhaps a few times, getting your score up to 85 or 90 percent. You're ready. Here are a few hints to get you successfully through the exam.

A few days or weeks before the state exam, find out exactly what you'll need to bring with you and find out what you can't bring with you. Permissible items change from time to time, so you need to check with the California Department of Real Estate or your course instructor on this. Admission into the exam may also change from time to time, so check out the necessary procedures and requirements to take the exam.

Typically, you'll need some or all of the following items:

- **Calculator:** I always bring two just in case. In California, students may only use a basic four-function calculator that does not have a printout capability or any alpha keys. Most real estate, financial, and scientific calculators are not acceptable for exam purposes. Additionally, cell-phone and PDA calculators are not allowed to be used during the examination.
- **Pencils:** The California DRE exam is not currently computerized. The examiner will supply pencils for the exam. Students are *not* encouraged to bring their own.
- **Identification:** A government issued photo ID is required; a DMV card, driver's license, or passport will suffice.
- **Permit:** You may need some kind of permit to take the exam. Check out the procedure and make sure you have whatever the state sends you to let you into the exam.

Make sure you eat your regular meals before the exam. Don't eat anything too heavy or different. If you think you'll get hungry, find out if you can bring food with you to the exam. If you have a medical condition that may require a snack during the period of the exam, get permission ahead of time in writing and bring it with you to the exam. DRE will allow bottled water and hard candy—but usually not sandwiches or other food items.

Don't bring anything with you that you won't need for the exam. Testing centers generally don't have places to safely put backpacks or briefcases and usually will not allow them into the exam room. Make sure not to bring your cell phone into the exam room; leave it at home or in your car trunk.

Prepare everything you'll need the night before and get a good night's sleep. Wake up in time to get to the testing center at least 15 to 30 minutes early and allow for traffic, finding a parking space, and mass-transit delays.

Finally, when you get to your seat, receive the exam and answer sheet, pay attention and follow the directions given to you by the exam proctor. The proctors are there to assist you. When you're ready to go, sit back for a minute, take a breath (or two or three), and relax. You're prepared and you've practiced by taking the tests in this book. Good luck and welcome to your new career!

PART II

PRACTICE TESTS

Answer Sheet for Practice Test 1

(Remove This Sheet and Use It to Mark Your Answers)

1 Ⓐ Ⓑ Ⓒ Ⓓ	21 Ⓐ Ⓑ Ⓒ Ⓓ	41 Ⓐ Ⓑ Ⓒ Ⓓ	61 Ⓐ Ⓑ Ⓒ Ⓓ
2 Ⓐ Ⓑ Ⓒ Ⓓ	22 Ⓐ Ⓑ Ⓒ Ⓓ	42 Ⓐ Ⓑ Ⓒ Ⓓ	62 Ⓐ Ⓑ Ⓒ Ⓓ
3 Ⓐ Ⓑ Ⓒ Ⓓ	23 Ⓐ Ⓑ Ⓒ Ⓓ	43 Ⓐ Ⓑ Ⓒ Ⓓ	63 Ⓐ Ⓑ Ⓒ Ⓓ
4 Ⓐ Ⓑ Ⓒ Ⓓ	24 Ⓐ Ⓑ Ⓒ Ⓓ	44 Ⓐ Ⓑ Ⓒ Ⓓ	64 Ⓐ Ⓑ Ⓒ Ⓓ
5 Ⓐ Ⓑ Ⓒ Ⓓ	25 Ⓐ Ⓑ Ⓒ Ⓓ	45 Ⓐ Ⓑ Ⓒ Ⓓ	65 Ⓐ Ⓑ Ⓒ Ⓓ
6 Ⓐ Ⓑ Ⓒ Ⓓ	26 Ⓐ Ⓑ Ⓒ Ⓓ	46 Ⓐ Ⓑ Ⓒ Ⓓ	66 Ⓐ Ⓑ Ⓒ Ⓓ
7 Ⓐ Ⓑ Ⓒ Ⓓ	27 Ⓐ Ⓑ Ⓒ Ⓓ	47 Ⓐ Ⓑ Ⓒ Ⓓ	67 Ⓐ Ⓑ Ⓒ Ⓓ
8 Ⓐ Ⓑ Ⓒ Ⓓ	28 Ⓐ Ⓑ Ⓒ Ⓓ	48 Ⓐ Ⓑ Ⓒ Ⓓ	68 Ⓐ Ⓑ Ⓒ Ⓓ
9 Ⓐ Ⓑ Ⓒ Ⓓ	29 Ⓐ Ⓑ Ⓒ Ⓓ	49 Ⓐ Ⓑ Ⓒ Ⓓ	69 Ⓐ Ⓑ Ⓒ Ⓓ
10 Ⓐ Ⓑ Ⓒ Ⓓ	30 Ⓐ Ⓑ Ⓒ Ⓓ	50 Ⓐ Ⓑ Ⓒ Ⓓ	70 Ⓐ Ⓑ Ⓒ Ⓓ
11 Ⓐ Ⓑ Ⓒ Ⓓ	31 Ⓐ Ⓑ Ⓒ Ⓓ	51 Ⓐ Ⓑ Ⓒ Ⓓ	71 Ⓐ Ⓑ Ⓒ Ⓓ
12 Ⓐ Ⓑ Ⓒ Ⓓ	32 Ⓐ Ⓑ Ⓒ Ⓓ	52 Ⓐ Ⓑ Ⓒ Ⓓ	72 Ⓐ Ⓑ Ⓒ Ⓓ
13 Ⓐ Ⓑ Ⓒ Ⓓ	33 Ⓐ Ⓑ Ⓒ Ⓓ	53 Ⓐ Ⓑ Ⓒ Ⓓ	73 Ⓐ Ⓑ Ⓒ Ⓓ
14 Ⓐ Ⓑ Ⓒ Ⓓ	34 Ⓐ Ⓑ Ⓒ Ⓓ	54 Ⓐ Ⓑ Ⓒ Ⓓ	74 Ⓐ Ⓑ Ⓒ Ⓓ
15 Ⓐ Ⓑ Ⓒ Ⓓ	35 Ⓐ Ⓑ Ⓒ Ⓓ	55 Ⓐ Ⓑ Ⓒ Ⓓ	75 Ⓐ Ⓑ Ⓒ Ⓓ
16 Ⓐ Ⓑ Ⓒ Ⓓ	36 Ⓐ Ⓑ Ⓒ Ⓓ	56 Ⓐ Ⓑ Ⓒ Ⓓ	76 Ⓐ Ⓑ Ⓒ Ⓓ
17 Ⓐ Ⓑ Ⓒ Ⓓ	37 Ⓐ Ⓑ Ⓒ Ⓓ	57 Ⓐ Ⓑ Ⓒ Ⓓ	77 Ⓐ Ⓑ Ⓒ Ⓓ
18 Ⓐ Ⓑ Ⓒ Ⓓ	38 Ⓐ Ⓑ Ⓒ Ⓓ	58 Ⓐ Ⓑ Ⓒ Ⓓ	78 Ⓐ Ⓑ Ⓒ Ⓓ
19 Ⓐ Ⓑ Ⓒ Ⓓ	39 Ⓐ Ⓑ Ⓒ Ⓓ	59 Ⓐ Ⓑ Ⓒ Ⓓ	79 Ⓐ Ⓑ Ⓒ Ⓓ
20 Ⓐ Ⓑ Ⓒ Ⓓ	40 Ⓐ Ⓑ Ⓒ Ⓓ	60 Ⓐ Ⓑ Ⓒ Ⓓ	80 Ⓐ Ⓑ Ⓒ Ⓓ

81 Ⓐ Ⓑ Ⓒ Ⓓ	101 Ⓐ Ⓑ Ⓒ Ⓓ	121 Ⓐ Ⓑ Ⓒ Ⓓ	141 Ⓐ Ⓑ Ⓒ Ⓓ
82 Ⓐ Ⓑ Ⓒ Ⓓ	102 Ⓐ Ⓑ Ⓒ Ⓓ	122 Ⓐ Ⓑ Ⓒ Ⓓ	142 Ⓐ Ⓑ Ⓒ Ⓓ
83 Ⓐ Ⓑ Ⓒ Ⓓ	103 Ⓐ Ⓑ Ⓒ Ⓓ	123 Ⓐ Ⓑ Ⓒ Ⓓ	143 Ⓐ Ⓑ Ⓒ Ⓓ
84 Ⓐ Ⓑ Ⓒ Ⓓ	104 Ⓐ Ⓑ Ⓒ Ⓓ	124 Ⓐ Ⓑ Ⓒ Ⓓ	144 Ⓐ Ⓑ Ⓒ Ⓓ
85 Ⓐ Ⓑ Ⓒ Ⓓ	105 Ⓐ Ⓑ Ⓒ Ⓓ	125 Ⓐ Ⓑ Ⓒ Ⓓ	145 Ⓐ Ⓑ Ⓒ Ⓓ
86 Ⓐ Ⓑ Ⓒ Ⓓ	106 Ⓐ Ⓑ Ⓒ Ⓓ	126 Ⓐ Ⓑ Ⓒ Ⓓ	146 Ⓐ Ⓑ Ⓒ Ⓓ
87 Ⓐ Ⓑ Ⓒ Ⓓ	107 Ⓐ Ⓑ Ⓒ Ⓓ	127 Ⓐ Ⓑ Ⓒ Ⓓ	147 Ⓐ Ⓑ Ⓒ Ⓓ
88 Ⓐ Ⓑ Ⓒ Ⓓ	108 Ⓐ Ⓑ Ⓒ Ⓓ	128 Ⓐ Ⓑ Ⓒ Ⓓ	148 Ⓐ Ⓑ Ⓒ Ⓓ
89 Ⓐ Ⓑ Ⓒ Ⓓ	109 Ⓐ Ⓑ Ⓒ Ⓓ	129 Ⓐ Ⓑ Ⓒ Ⓓ	149 Ⓐ Ⓑ Ⓒ Ⓓ
90 Ⓐ Ⓑ Ⓒ Ⓓ	110 Ⓐ Ⓑ Ⓒ Ⓓ	130 Ⓐ Ⓑ Ⓒ Ⓓ	150 Ⓐ Ⓑ Ⓒ Ⓓ
91 Ⓐ Ⓑ Ⓒ Ⓓ	111 Ⓐ Ⓑ Ⓒ Ⓓ	131 Ⓐ Ⓑ Ⓒ Ⓓ	
92 Ⓐ Ⓑ Ⓒ Ⓓ	112 Ⓐ Ⓑ Ⓒ Ⓓ	132 Ⓐ Ⓑ Ⓒ Ⓓ	
93 Ⓐ Ⓑ Ⓒ Ⓓ	113 Ⓐ Ⓑ Ⓒ Ⓓ	133 Ⓐ Ⓑ Ⓒ Ⓓ	
94 Ⓐ Ⓑ Ⓒ Ⓓ	114 Ⓐ Ⓑ Ⓒ Ⓓ	134 Ⓐ Ⓑ Ⓒ Ⓓ	
95 Ⓐ Ⓑ Ⓒ Ⓓ	115 Ⓐ Ⓑ Ⓒ Ⓓ	135 Ⓐ Ⓑ Ⓒ Ⓓ	
96 Ⓐ Ⓑ Ⓒ Ⓓ	116 Ⓐ Ⓑ Ⓒ Ⓓ	136 Ⓐ Ⓑ Ⓒ Ⓓ	
97 Ⓐ Ⓑ Ⓒ Ⓓ	117 Ⓐ Ⓑ Ⓒ Ⓓ	137 Ⓐ Ⓑ Ⓒ Ⓓ	
98 Ⓐ Ⓑ Ⓒ Ⓓ	118 Ⓐ Ⓑ Ⓒ Ⓓ	138 Ⓐ Ⓑ Ⓒ Ⓓ	
99 Ⓐ Ⓑ Ⓒ Ⓓ	119 Ⓐ Ⓑ Ⓒ Ⓓ	139 Ⓐ Ⓑ Ⓒ Ⓓ	
100 Ⓐ Ⓑ Ⓒ Ⓓ	120 Ⓐ Ⓑ Ⓒ Ⓓ	140 Ⓐ Ⓑ Ⓒ Ⓓ	

Practice Test 1

Directions: For each of the following questions, select the choice that best answers the question.

1. The term that best describes a continuous urban corridor joining at least two cities is

   A. megalopolis.
   B. standard metropolitan statistical area.
   C. metropolitan area.
   D. standard urban area.

2. The term *real property* can also be described as

   A. personal property.
   B. the bundle of rights.
   C. chattels.
   D. land.

3. The rights of a landowner to a river bordering her property are known as

   A. littoral rights.
   B. correlative use rights.
   C. riparian rights.
   D. rights of appropriation.

4. In the case of a transfer of ownership of a piece of real estate, a fixture is normally

   A. assumed to be included in the transfer.
   B. assumed to remain with the original owner.
   C. transferred only if there is an agreement.
   D. subject to a separate bill of sale.

5. A tenant who operates a jewelry store wants to take his jewelry cases with him at the expiration of the lease. Which of the following is most correct?

   A. He may take the jewelry cases.
   B. He may not take the jewelry cases.
   C. He may take the cases only if he has a prior agreement with the landlord.
   D. He may take the cases if removal will not cause substantial damage.

6. A legal description of property is not adequate unless

   A. a street address is included.
   B. at least two different methods are used.
   C. it includes a detailed description of the structures.
   D. none of the above

GO ON TO THE NEXT PAGE

7. The lot and block system of property description is not also known as the

   A. lot, block, and tract system.
   B. subdivision system.
   C. rectangular survey system.
   D. plat map system.

8. How many acres does a section of land contain?

   A. 40
   B. 160
   C. 320
   D. 640

9. The type of ownership that provides the most complete bundle of rights is

   A. fee simple qualified.
   B. fee simple absolute.
   C. fee simple defeasible.
   D. fee simple freehold.

10. Which of the following best describes the interests of the holder of a life estate?

   A. possession
   B. possession and use
   C. possession, use, and ownership
   D. possession, use, and ownership—but only as long as they live

11. The requirement that multiple owners take title to property at the same time is a characteristic of

   A. ownership in severalty.
   B. joint tenancy.
   C. tenancy in common.
   D. all forms of concurrent ownership.

12. Which of the following are most similar to each other with respect to inheriting property?

   A. joint tenancy and community property with right of survivorship
   B. joint tenancy and tenancy in common
   C. tenancy in common and community property with right of survivorship
   D. joint tenancy and community property

13. Which of the following is a generic term for a group of people joining together to invest in real estate?

   A. corporation
   B. real estate investment trust
   C. limited partnership
   D. syndicate

14. When is a landowner entitled to compensation for a change in zoning?

   A. when the landowner is denied all practical economic use of the property
   B. when the property loses value
   C. when the property increases in value
   D. The property owner is never entitled to compensation.

15. A statement of the goals and policies regarding growth of a community is a good definition of the

   A. zoning ordinance.
   B. general plan.
   C. specific plan.
   D. subdivision regulations.

16. The proper way for a landowner who has physical difficulty in developing his property to get relief is to obtain a

   A. rezoning.
   B. conditional use permit.
   C. master plan amendment.
   D. variance.

17. At which lot does the Subdivided Lands Law take effect?

   A. the first lot
   B. the third lot
   C. the fifth lot
   D. the tenth lot

18. The primary difference between a common interest subdivision and a standard subdivision is

   A. design.
   B. ownership of common areas.
   C. use restrictions.
   D. parcel size.

GO ON TO THE NEXT PAGE

19. The state has enacted legislation providing special consideration or control for development of

    A. rangeland.
    B. earthquake areas.
    C. coastal areas.
    D. all of the above

20. All liens are encumbrances. All encumbrances are

    A. liens.
    B. limitations.
    C. voluntary.
    D. involuntary.

21. A mechanic's lien creates

    A. a cloud on title.
    B. a marketable title.
    C. a transferable title.
    D. no problem in transferring title.

22. The land that benefits from an easement is referred to as the

    A. servient tenement.
    B. dominant tenement.
    C. appurtenant tenement.
    D. gross tenement.

23. A deed restriction prohibiting the sale of property to certain ethnic groups

    A. is enforceable only if the restriction predates civil rights laws.
    B. is enforceable in subdivisions of fewer than five lots.
    C. supersedes civil rights laws.
    D. is illegal and unenforceable.

24. A private deed restriction that places a restraint on alienation

    A. is void.
    B. restricts the sale of property.
    C. is unenforceable.
    D. all of the above

25. The process by which eminent domain occurs is called

    A. alienation.

    B. inverse condemnation.

    C. police power.

    D. condemnation.

26. Which of the following types of easement does not run with the land?

    A. the electric company's easement to cross over your land with their power lines

    B. a driveway easement allowing your neighbor to cross your property to get to the highway

    C. an underground waterline easement across your property for your neighbor to obtain water from the street main

    D. an agreement to allow your neighbor to use your property to park cars on the day of his daughter's wedding

27. An easement is an encumbrance

    A. only if it has no time limit.

    B. only if it is an easement appurtenant.

    C. only if it is an easement in gross.

    D. always.

28. An agent represents a

    A. buyer.

    B. seller.

    C. customer.

    D. principal.

29. What is another term for an agent entrusted to act on someone's behalf?

    A. subagent

    B. surrogate

    C. fiduciary

    D. cooperating agent

30. The seller of a one-family house is required to disclose to buyers

    A. the fact that the last occupant died of AIDS.

    B. the structural and mechanical condition of the property.

    C. information about a murder that occurred in the house ten years earlier.

    D. the fact that the buyers are the original owners of the property.

GO ON TO THE NEXT PAGE

31. The agent who brings a ready, willing, and able buyer to a seller is commonly called the

    A. buyer's agent.

    B. seller's agent.

    C. procuring cause.

    D. fiduciary.

32. Broker A has a listing agreement to sell Seller B's house. Broker A brings an offer to Seller B on behalf of Buyer C. Seller B rejects the offer and a week later attempts to negotiate directly with Buyer C. Seller B has violated

    A. the duty of care.

    B. the duty of loyalty.

    C. the duty of confidentiality.

    D. obedience.

33. Seller A has signed a listing agreement with Broker B. Without the assistance of Broker B, Seller A sells her property and under the terms of the listing agreement owes no commission to Broker B. What type of listing agreement did Seller A sign?

    A. a net listing

    B. an exclusive authorization and right to sell listing

    C. an option listing

    D. an exclusive agency listing

34. Broker A agrees to represent Seller B in the sale of her house. Seller B agrees to pay Broker A a commission if he successfully sells the house. What do we know for certain based on these facts?

    A. Broker A has an exclusive authorization and right-to-sell listing agreement.

    B. A unilateral express contract exists between Broker A and Seller B.

    C. Broker A has an exclusive agency agreement with the seller.

    D. A bilateral express contract exists between Broker A and Seller B.

35. Seller A wants to walk away with $200,000 after the sale of her house and all expenses are paid. She agrees that Broker B can keep, as his fee, anything he gets above that. What type of agreement have they made?

    A. a net listing

    B. an option listing

    C. an exclusive agency listing

    D. an open listing

36. A cooperating broker may represent

    A. the buyer.

    B. the seller.

    C. the listing broker.

    D. any of the above

37. Who of the following owes fiduciary responsibility to the buyer?

    A. the seller's agent

    B. the buyer's agent

    C. the subagent of the seller

    D. the subagent of the seller's agent

38. A real estate salesperson is always considered an

    A. employee.

    B. independent contractor.

    C. agent of the buyer.

    D. agent of the seller.

39. Which of the following is not a type of listing agreement?

    A. open listing

    B. multiple listing

    C. net listing

    D. exclusive agency listing

40. A broker hired to sell a house is considered a

    A. universal agent.

    B. general agent.

    C. special agent.

    D. limited agent.

41. Seller A wants to get the broadest exposure for the sale of her house but does not want to pay a commission if she sells the house herself. What type of listing will she try to establish?

    A. open listing

    B. pocket listing

    C. multiple listing

    D. exclusive authorization and right-to-sell listing

42. Broker A has a listing to market Seller B's house. He also has a buyer's agency agreement to find a house for Buyer C. If Buyer C becomes interested in Seller B's house what might the danger be, if any, to Broker A?

    A. none

    B. the creation of an open listing

    C. a potential conflict of interest

    D. the creation of a dual agency

GO ON TO THE NEXT PAGE

43. All agency agreements for the sale of property must be in writing except creation of an agency by

    A. implied agreement.

    B. estoppel.

    C. ratification.

    D. There are no exceptions.

44. Broker A agrees in writing to keep details of Seller B's property in his files but indicated that he will not actively market it. Seller B agrees to pay Broker A a commission if he finds a buyer. This agreement would best be described as

    A. express bilateral.

    B. express unilateral.

    C. implied bilateral.

    D. implied unilateral.

45. An uncashed deposit check usually may be held and not deposited by the broker for how many days before an offer is accepted?

    A. three

    B. five

    C. seven

    D. until the offer is accepted

46. The most profitable single use that will generate the highest value for a piece of property is called its

    A. economical use.

    B. feasible use.

    C. highest and best use.

    D. anticipated use.

47. Which of the following is not a characteristic of value?

    A. change

    B. utility

    C. transferability

    D. demand

48. Two lots, each valued at $50,000, when combined have a value of $125,000. What term best describes this added value?

    A. supply and demand

    B. substitution

    C. utility

    D. plottage

49. In appraising a property, the process by which dissimilarities are accounted for in comparing a subject property and a comparable property is called

   A. reconciling the values.
   B. making adjustments.
   C. equalization.
   D. estimating value.

50. Which of the following is an example of functional obsolescence?

   A. having to get to a bedroom by going through another bedroom
   B. a gas station located next to a house
   C. a house badly in need of exterior painting
   D. a house located within walking distance of a train station

51. Which of the following is deducted from potential gross income to arrive at effective gross income?

   A. operating expenses
   B. debt service
   C. vacancy and collection loss
   D. all of the above

52. An appraisal may have more than one date on it. The date of the value estimate is the

   A. inspection date.
   B. effective date.
   C. report date.
   D. certification date.

53. If you assume that depreciation occurs at an even rate, what method of calculating depreciation would you be using?

   A. economic age life method
   B. breakdown method
   C. market extraction method
   D. index method

54. In the income approach to estimating value, another term for the capitalization rate is

   A. before-tax cash-flow rate.
   B. cash-on-cash rate.
   C. expense ratio.
   D. rate of return.

GO ON TO THE NEXT PAGE

55. A parking lot in a downtown area being developed with office buildings is most likely

    A. the highest and best use of the property.

    B. an interim use of the property.

    C. an economically feasible use of the property.

    D. the best use of the property.

56. The gross rent multiplier approach is a useful income approach in appraising

    A. special-purpose buildings like churches.

    B. retail shopping malls.

    C. office buildings.

    D. single-family homes.

57. In order to arrive at a final value estimate after applying all three approaches to value, which of the following will an appraiser do?

    A. Average the three values.

    B. Reconcile the three values.

    C. Adjust the three values so that they're equal.

    D. Select the value closest to the sale price.

58. Potential gross income of an investment property is the same as

    A. scheduled rent plus other building income.

    B. current rent only.

    C. market rent plus other building income.

    D. market rent only.

59. Which approach to valuation estimates land and building value separately?

    A. cost approach

    B. income capitalization approach

    C. sales comparison approach

    D. gross rent multiplier approach

60. What type of value is the term *ad valorem* most closely associated with?

    A. investment value

    B. assessed value

    C. market value

    D. depreciated value

61. Appraisers paid on the basis of a percentage of the value of a property are

A. called fee appraisers.
B. usually only employed by banks and mortgage companies.
C. employed by investors to guarantee the most accurate appraised value.
D. in violation of appraisal ethical standards.

62. "An improvement to a property is worth the value it adds, if any, to the whole property, not its individual cost or value" is a good definition of the principle of

A. conformity.
B. change.
C. anticipation.
D. contribution.

63. Rising mortgage interest rates will tend to

A. lower property values.
B. raise property values.
C. have no effect on property value.
D. only affect appraised but not actual values.

64. A person wanting to buy a $200,000 home by putting down $40,000 in cash and borrowing $160,000 is making use of what financial concept?

A. leverage
B. equity yield
C. total yield
D. discount rate

65. A buyer purchases a $275,000 house with $60,000 down and a mortgage loan of $215,000. In order to secure a preferred interest rate, the borrower must pay the bank 1 point. How much will this charge be?

A. $27,500
B. $21,500
C. $2,150
D. $600

66. Which of the following activities of the Federal Reserve System is likely to have the most direct effect on the rates charged for consumer credit?

A. adjusting the reserve requirements
B. selling securities to raise funds
C. adjusting the discount rate
D. increasing the number of loans made to consumers

GO ON TO THE NEXT PAGE

67. After 1989, who insured deposits in all federally chartered banks?

    A. FIRREA

    B. FDIC

    C. FHA

    D. FHLLB

68. "The difference between the value of a property and all debts attributed to it" is a good definition of

    A. leverage.

    B. LTV.

    C. discounting.

    D. equity.

69. The terms and conditions of the promise to pay back money borrowed to buy a house is found in the

    A. mortgage.

    B. trust deed

    C. promissory note.

    D. deed of trust.

70. The process by which a mortgage loan is paid off in equal payments consisting of principal and interest is called

    A. discounting.

    B. amortization.

    C. a term loan.

    D. an equity loan.

71. The object of creating a negotiable instrument is to

    A. allow a note to be transferred.

    B. be able to foreclose on the property.

    C. make sure payment is made.

    D. avoid foreclosure.

72. A home buyer borrows $280,000 to purchase a home for 30 years at an interest rate of 7%. How much interest will he pay the first year on the loan?

    A. $19,600

    B. $5,599

    C. $1,634

    D. Not enough information is provided.

73. California law protects homeowners when the sale of the property cannot cover the outstanding mortgage balance

A. under all circumstances.
B. only when the home has been owned for at least two years.
C. only on refinancing loans.
D. only on the original purchase mortgage loan.

74. A purchaser wants to buy a house that costs $330,000. The bank is offering a mortgage loan at a loan-to-value ratio of 80%. How much will the purchaser need for a down payment?

A. $330,000
B. $264,000
C. $66,000
D. $33,000

75. What does a discount point do to the effective yield that a lender gets from a mortgage loan?

A. It raises it.
B. It has no effect.
C. It lowers it.
D. It lowers it, but only if the seller, not the buyer, pays it.

76. Equity is most accurately defined as

A. the sale price of the house minus the mortgage amount.
B. the value of the house minus all liens and encumbrances.
C. the value of the house minus the mortgage.
D. the amount of the down payment.

77. The law that controls advertising of real estate loans is

A. RESPA
B. ECOA
C. Regulation Z
D. FIRREA

78. A mortgage lender requires a borrower to make monthly payments, in addition to the mortgage payments, to a special account to cover taxes and hazard insurance costs for the property. This type of account is commonly called

A. a savings account.
B. a tax account.
C. an impound account.
D. a takeout account.

GO ON TO THE NEXT PAGE

79. Which of the following is not true of VA and FHA loan programs in California?

   A. Loans are guaranteed or insured by these agencies.

   B. Special qualifications or limits exist for these programs.

   C. Both programs allow adjustable-rate mortgages.

   D. Money is lent directly by these agencies.

80. Which type of mortgage loan typically results in negative amortization?

   A. fixed rate

   B. adjustable rate

   C. growing equity

   D. graduated payment

81. A type of purchase financing that allows the seller to take immediate possession of the property but delays transfer of title is

   A. a land contract.

   B. a contract for deed.

   C. an installment sales contract.

   D. all of the above

82. The interest rate charged by the Federal Reserve System to borrow money is called the

   A. open market rate.

   B. prime rate.

   C. discount rate.

   D. reserve rate.

83. Buyer A pays $300,000 for a house putting down $60,000 and borrowing $240,000. The house appreciates 25% during the years he owns it. When he sells the house, what is his profit?

   A. $15,000

   B. $75,000

   C. $135,000

   D. $375,000

84. A testator who dies testate has no need of

   A. the laws of intestate succession.

   B. a will.

   C. probate.

   D. the laws of accession.

85. Which of the following is true?

    A. All accessions are accretions.
    B. All accretions are accessions.
    C. All accessions are improvements.
    D. All accessions are fixtures.

86. Builder A turns over the streets in his new subdivision to the town. He does this by

    A. private grant.
    B. common law dedication.
    C. public grant.
    D. statutory dedication.

87. Whose signature must be on a deed to make it valid?

    A. the grantee
    B. the grantor
    C. the grantor and the grantee
    D. two witnesses

88. Extra protection for title problems on property conveyed by a warranty deed is provided by

    A. the acknowledgment.
    B. the signature of the grantee.
    C. the granting clause.
    D. title insurance.

89. The creation of escrow is conditional on

    A. a meeting of the minds.
    B. procurement of a ready, willing, and able buyer.
    C. execution of a binding contract.
    D. creation of a settlement statement.

90. Which of the following is not a duty of an escrow agent?

    A. to disclose pertinent material facts
    B. to prepare settlement statements
    C. to bring an interpleader legal action if necessary
    D. to conduct an independent investigation of the transaction

GO ON TO THE NEXT PAGE

Practice Test 1

91. The process by which payments such as taxes are allocated at closing is called

    A. proration.
    B. distribution.
    C. accounting.
    D. settlement.

92. A seller has paid taxes of $2,400 in advance on July 1 for the following year. He closes sale of the property on November 1. Who owes how much to whom?

    A. The seller owes the buyer $1,400.
    B. The buyer owes the seller $1,400.
    C. The seller owes the buyer $1,200.
    D. The buyer owes the seller $1,200.

93. The opposite of *marketable title* can best be expressed as

    A. good title.
    B. chain of title.
    C. abstract of title.
    D. cloud on title.

94. Which of the following is true regarding title insurance policy coverage for changes in land use as a result of zoning changes?

    A. It is covered by CLTA extended coverage policy.
    B. It is covered by ALTA extended coverage policy.
    C. It is not covered by either ALTA or CLTA extended coverage policy.
    D. It is covered by both standard and extended coverage policies.

95. The term *ad valorem* usually is associated with

    A. income taxes.
    B. property taxes.
    C. corporation taxes.
    D. estate taxes.

96. Assuming that the current assessed value of a property after all exemptions have been applied is $55,000, what is the annual tax on that property?

    A. $55
    B. $550
    C. $5,500
    D. $2,250

97. What is the term used to describe the depositing of a client's funds into the broker's personal or business account?

A. commingling
B. mixing
C. accounting
D. escrow

98. What is the most desirable form of deposit from a seller's point of view?

A. a demand note
B. a postdated check
C. an immediately negotiable check
D. All of the above are the same.

99. The act that extended antidiscrimination protection to business establishments is the

A. Federal Fair Housing Act.
B. Housing Financial Discrimination Act.
C. Unruh Civil Rights Act.
D. Fair Employment and Housing Act.

100. The California law that specifically prohibits redlining is the

A. Housing Financial Discrimination Act.
B. Unruh Civil Rights Act.
C. Fair Employments and Housing Act.
D. Rumford Fair Housing Act.

101. Blind ads for real estate are permitted

A. for all properties.
B. for no properties.
C. for mobile homes only.
D. when the owner wants to remain anonymous.

102. A mobile home advertisement must be withdrawn within how many hours of the home being taken off the market?

A. 12
B. 24
C. 48
D. 72

GO ON TO THE NEXT PAGE

27

103. A broker must maintain records of a transaction for how many years from the date of closing?

    A. 1

    B. 2

    C. 3

    D. 5

104. A broker who employs salespeople as independent contractors rather than employees has

    A. less supervisory responsibility.

    B. more supervisory responsibility.

    C. the same amount of supervisory responsibility.

    D. no supervisory responsibility.

105. A salesperson collects a commission directly from a homeowner after selling her house. Which of the following is true?

    A. The salesperson has violated the law.

    B. The salesperson can accept the commission.

    C. The salesperson can accept the commission as long as he shares an appropriate amount with his broker.

    D. The salesperson may accept the commission, but only if he is an independent contractor rather than an employee.

106. Which of the following activities could be performed by an unlicensed assistant?

    A. cold-calling to solicit listings

    B. contacting owners who have open listings to secure an exclusive listing

    C. creating sales brochures

    D. leasing activities on behalf of several building owners

107. Real estate law in California is administered by the

    A. Department of Real Estate.

    B. Department of State.

    C. Attorney General.

    D. Real Estate Advisory Commission.

108. A violation of the Real Estate Law could result in all of the following penalties except

    A. a fine.

    B. license suspension.

    C. license revocation.

    D. a term of not more than one year in jail.

109. An unpaid child support obligation will result in what type of license being issued to a real estate salesperson applicant?

A. a 30-day temporary license

B. a 90-day temporary license

C. a 120-day temporary license

D. a 150-day temporary license

110. Which of the following is not exempt from requiring a real estate license?

A. a resident property manager

B. a personal property broker

C. a vacation home rental agent

D. a corporation providing real estate sales services

111. Payments for a financial injury sustained by a person as a result of the fraudulent practices of a real estate broker would be made from the

A. California Association of Realtors.

B. California Real Estate Recovery Fund.

C. California Pooled Money Investment Fund.

D. California Residential Mortgage Lending Act.

112. Which of the following statements is true?

A. All real estate licensees are Realtors.

B. All real estate licensees are Realtists.

C. All real estate licensees are subject to the State Code of Real Estate Ethics.

D. none of the above

113. Informed consent to practice dual agency is

A. required by California law only.

B. required by the National Association of Realtors code of ethics only.

C. required by both California law and the National Association of Realtors code of ethics.

D. not required.

114. When must a real estate salesperson be licensed in order to receive a commission?

A. at the time of the transaction

B. at least 30 days before the transaction

C. within 30 days of the transaction

D. none of the above, as long as the broker is licensed

GO ON TO THE NEXT PAGE

115. How long does an applicant have from the time of passing the license exam to obtain his salesperson license?

    A. six months

    B. one year

    C. 18 months

    D. two years

116. Which of the following is true?

    A. All brokers are Realtors.

    B. All salespeople must work for brokers.

    C. All Realtors are salespeople.

    D. All Realtors are brokers.

117. The grace period during which an expired license may be renewed simply by paying a renewal fee is

    A. two years, and the agent can practice during that time.

    B. two years, and the agent cannot practice during that time.

    C. one year, and the agent can practice during that time.

    D. one year, and the agent cannot practice during that time.

118. Commercial property owners may require a maximum of

    A. three months' rent as security.

    B. six months' rent as security.

    C. 10% of the total lease amount as security.

    D. There is no maximum.

119. Public improvements such as sidewalks may be paid for by

    A. *ad valorem* taxes.

    B. Mello-Roos Community Facilities Act bonds.

    C. special assessments.

    D. all of the above

120. The agent conducting the mandatory physical inspection of the property certifies the completion of the inspection in

    A. the inspection certification.

    B. HUD-1 Form.

    C. the FNMA report form.

    D. the Real Estate Transfer Disclosure Statement.

121. Buyer A is interested in purchasing a property from an estate. He asks the broker how the previous owner died. The owner died 18 months ago by suicide. The broker

   A. must answer the question honestly.

   B. may not reveal the information.

   C. may reveal the information if he wants to.

   D. must obtain the family's permission to reveal the information.

122. Seller disclosure of a dwelling's physical condition is required of

   A. retail property.

   B. commercial property.

   C. mobile homes.

   D. residential property of five units or more.

123. Within what time frame must a legal action be filed as a result of information in a property transfer disclosure statement?

   A. six months

   B. one year

   C. two years

   D. three years

124. The Real Estate Recovery Account is funded from

   A. *ad valorem* taxes.

   B. Mello-Roos assessments.

   C. the California Board of Realtors.

   D. real estate license fees.

125. A house is being sold by a real estate broker on behalf of a homeowner. The basement leaks every time there's more than an inch of rain. The house is on a substandard-size lot, which will require a zoning variance to make any additions. The school district is rated in the bottom half of all districts in the state. And the furnace is 20 years old. Which of the following statements is least likely to be considered fraudulent misrepresentation?

   A. This house is in a great school district.

   B. You shouldn't have any water problems in the basement.

   C. The furnace is pretty new.

   D. You'll have no problem adding on to the house.

126. Broker A is selling property to Buyer B. In which, if any, of the following situations would Broker A have to disclose his interest?

   A. Broker A's brother-in-law owns the property.

   B. Broker A owns the property.

   C. Corporation C owns the property and Broker A is part owner of the corporation.

   D. all of the above

GO ON TO THE NEXT PAGE

127. A member of the National Association of Realtors is known as a

    A. broker.
    B. realtist.
    C. Realtor.
    D. real estate agent.

128. The Homeowner's Guide to Earthquake Safety must be provided to purchasers of one- to four-family homes built prior to

    A. January 1, 1960.
    B. December 31, 1960.
    C. January 1, 1978.
    D. December 31, 1978.

129. For disclosure purposes, a material fact effecting property value would include all but which of the following?

    A. an environmental hazard located on the property
    B. an environmental hazard located 500 feet from the property
    C. the presence of a significant minority population in the community
    D. the fact that the house is built on a smaller-than-permitted lot

130. Houses built after 1980 and sold with the assistance of a broker will require all of the following except

    A. a lead-paint hazard disclosure.
    B. a Mello-Roos lien disclosure.
    C. a real estate transfer disclosure statement.
    D. an agency disclosure.

131. With respect to disclosure, state responsibility areas deal with

    A. flood hazard.
    B. fire hazard.
    C. mudslide hazard.
    D. seismic hazard.

132. Ordnance location disclosure deals with the

    A. existence of special coastal zone regulations.
    B. presence of possible building code violations in a structure.
    C. likelihood of fire hazard in the area.
    D. possibility of live ammunition from military installations in the area.

133. One party agrees to sell another party a piece of property in exchange for a certain amount of money. The agreement is in writing. What type of contract do the parties have?

    A. express bilateral

    B. express unilateral

    C. implied bilateral

    D. implied unilateral

134. Owner A hires someone to burn down his building for the insurance money. They agree on all the terms including payment. The contract would be

    A. valid.

    B. void.

    C. voidable.

    D. unenforceable.

135. An option to purchase property is considered an

    A. express bilateral agreement.

    B. express unilateral agreement.

    C. implied bilateral agreement.

    D. implied unilateral agreement.

136. Which of the following types of listing agreements need not be in writing?

    A. an agent representing a buyer purchasing a home

    B. an agent representing a seller selling commercial property

    C. an agent representing a seller of vacant land when the agent also has an option to purchase the property

    D. an agent representing a landlord renting rooms in a rooming house on a week-to-week basis

137. A real estate broker always represents the principal, who is always the

    A. seller.

    B. buyer.

    C. customer.

    D. buyer and/or seller.

138. At what phase of the contract process is a real estate commission generally earned?

    A. submission of deposit

    B. agreement of terms

    C. mutual consent

    D. deposit placed in a trust account

GO ON TO THE NEXT PAGE

139. Buyer A indicates to Seller B that he wants to purchase Seller B's property for $300,000. Seller B tells Buyer A that he would be willing to sell the property for $350,000. At this point, which of the following is correct?

   A. Buyer A is the offeror; Seller B is the offeree.

   B. Buyer A is the offeree; Seller B is the offeror.

   C. Buyer A is the grantee; Seller B is the grantor.

   D. Buyer A is the trustee; Seller B is the beneficiary.

140. What is the minimum age for a married person to enter into a contract?

   A. 18

   B. 19

   C. 21

   D. There is no minimum age for a married person.

141. In an option agreement, the consideration is

   A. the amount to be paid for the property.

   B. 10% of the amount to be paid for the property.

   C. the amount paid for the right to purchase the property.

   D. refundable if the option is not exercised.

142. An exclusive authorization and right-to-sell agreement is considered an

   A. implied unilateral contract.

   B. express unilateral contract.

   C. implied bilateral contract.

   D. express bilateral contract.

143. A tenant who stays in rented property after the lease has expired without the consent of the landlord is said to have

   A. an estate at sufferance.

   B. an estate at will.

   C. a periodic estate.

   D. an estate for years.

144. The tenant's interest in property is a

   A. leased fee and is considered real property.

   B. leasehold and is considered personal property.

   C. leased fee and is considered personal property.

   D. leasehold and is considered real property.

145. A periodic tenancy can be created from some other type of tenancy

    A. by agreement.
    B. by the landlord accepting the rent.
    C. neither A nor B
    D. either A or B

146. In addition to providing the services contracted for, what one thing is necessary for a commission payment to be enforced as a result of the listing agreement?

    A. The salesperson must have been licensed at the time of the transaction.
    B. The agreement must be in writing.
    C. The statement of services, such as advertising, must be clearly stated.
    D. The date of payment must be stated.

147. Broker A receives two offers on Seller B's house, which is listed for sale at $250,000. The first offer is for all cash at $200,000. The second offer is for 20% down with 80% financing for the full price. What should the broker do with respect to both offers?

    A. Present both offers to the seller as soon as possible.
    B. Present only the first offer to the seller, because it's an all-cash offer and will result in a fast closing.
    C. Present only the second offer to the seller, because it's for the full price.
    D. Hold the offers for a week or so to see if more offers are made.

148. The Mobilehome Residency Law covers agreements

    A. between management and resident owners.
    B. between management and nonresident owners.
    C. between management and tenants in a park-owned home.
    D. both A and B

149. The charging of interest on a note that is in excess of the statutory maximum rate is called

    A. a balloon loan.
    B. the index.
    C. an adjustable-rate loan.
    D. usury.

150. The two primary documents dealing with payment of a loan are the mortgage or deed of trust and a

    A. promissory note.
    B. survey.
    C. legal description.
    D. sales contract.

Answer Key for Practice Test 1

1. A	**36.** D	**71.** A
2. B	**37.** B	**72.** A
3. C	**38.** A	**73.** D
4. A	**39.** B	**74.** C
5. D	**40.** C	**75.** A
6. D	**41.** A	**76.** B
7. C	**42.** D	**77.** C
8. D	**43.** D	**78.** C
9. B	**44.** B	**79.** D
10. C	**45.** D	**80.** D
11. B	**46.** C	**81.** D
12. A	**47.** A	**82.** C
13. D	**48.** D	**83.** B
14. A	**49.** B	**84.** A
15. B	**50.** A	**85.** B
16. D	**51.** C	**86.** D
17. C	**52.** B	**87.** B
18. B	**53.** A	**88.** D
19. D	**54.** D	**89.** C
20. B	**55.** B	**90.** D
21. A	**56.** D	**91.** A
22. B	**57.** B	**92.** B
23. D	**58.** C	**93.** D
24. D	**59.** A	**94.** C
25. D	**60.** B	**95.** B
26. A	**61.** D	**96.** B
27. D	**62.** D	**97.** A
28. D	**63.** A	**98.** C
29. C	**64.** A	**99.** C
30. B	**65.** C	**100.** A
31. C	**66.** C	**101.** B
32. A	**67.** B	**102.** C
33. D	**68.** D	**103.** C
34. D	**69.** C	**104.** C
35. A	**70.** B	**105.** A

106. C	**121.** A	**136.** D
107. A	**122.** C	**137.** D
108. D	**123.** D	**138.** C
109. D	**124.** D	**139.** B
110. D	**125.** A	**140.** D
111. B	**126.** D	**141.** C
112. D	**127.** C	**142.** D
113. C	**128.** A	**143.** A
114. A	**129.** C	**144.** B
115. B	**130.** A	**145.** D
116. B	**131.** B	**146.** B
117. B	**132.** D	**147.** A
118. D	**133.** A	**148.** D
119. D	**134.** B	**149.** D
120. D	**135.** B	**150.** A

Answers and Explanations for Practice Test 1

1. **A.** This is the standard term used to describe a continuous urban area where urbanization has filled in the space between cities.

2. **B.** Choices A and C are definitely wrong, because *chattel* is another term for personal property. The term *land* is usually used to describe the physical surface of the Earth and all that it comprises including minerals and soil; it is not used to describe the rights of ownership.

3. **C.** Littorial rights refer to still bodies of water. The right of appropriation has to do with state rights, and correlative use relates to underground water use.

4. **A.** A fixture is normally included in the transfer of ownership unless there is an agreement to the contrary.

5. **D.** This is the most correct answer, given the information. Trade fixtures normally belong to the tenant and may be removed unless otherwise stated in the lease, but the damage must not be substantial or be able to be easily repaired.

6. **D.** A street address may not be available for rural properties. One method is sufficient, though sometimes two methods are combined. Legal descriptions define land boundaries, so specific structures are not part of the description.

7. **C.** The rectangular survey system is a different system of legal description.

8. **D.** This is something you'll have to memorize.

9. **B.** The other forms of ownership can or do have some type of limitation.

10. **C.** The holder of a life estate has no fee ownership interest but has possession and use.

11. **B.** Taking title at the same time is a feature of joint tenancy not the other forms mentioned.

12. **A.** Joint tenancy and community property with right of survivorship provide for complete reversion of the property interest to the remaining owner(s).

13. **D.** It's important here to understand the meaning of the term *generic*. *Generic* means "general" or "all-encompassing." A real estate syndicate may be formed as any one of the other forms mentioned in the answer choices.

14. **A.** A property owner is entitled to compensation if the land loses all of its practical value for development or use.

15. **B.** All of the incorrect answers control and guide growth in some way, but the general statement of policies and goals for a community is contained in the general plan, also called the master plan.

16. **D.** Where the owner of a single lot has practical difficulty in developing that lot a variance is most appropriate.

17. **C.** The Subdivided Lands Law takes effect on five or more parcels of land.

18. **B.** The principle characteristic of a common-interest subdivision is the existence of property owned commonly by the owners.

19. **D.** Special programs have been adopted to deal with or protect all of these areas.

20. **B.** Choice B is the only completely true statement. All encumbrances are some form of limitation on title or property use.

21. **A.** All liens tend to create clouds on titles, some more easily resolved than others.

22. **B.** This is definitional. Choices C and D use words associated with easements but do not describe the interest of the party benefiting from the easement.

23. **D.** The object of a deed restriction must be legal.

24. **D.** A private deed restriction that causes a restraint on alienation that interferes with a person's right to freely transfer title to the property is void and, therefore, unenforceable.

25. D. The police power grants the government the right of eminent domain, but the process by which it is implemented is called condemnation.

26. A. This is an easement in gross, which does not run with the land. Choice D is actually a permit or license and not an easement at all. The other two answer choices are easements appurtenant.

27. D. Because all easements are limitations on the use of land, they are always considered encumbrances.

28. D. The agent may represent a buyer or seller but always represents the principal.

29. C. You could argue that choices A and B have some qualities of representation, but in the context of real estate work, an agent is a fiduciary.

30. B. Owners of one- to four-unit dwellings must complete a disclosure statement about the property's physical condition.

31. C. The procuring cause is the agent who is successful at bringing the buyer and seller together.

32. A. Although fiduciary duties are generally owed by the agent to the principal the duty of care—that is, not interfering with the business of the agent—is owed by the principal to the agent.

33. D. You could get creative and think of ways the seller would owe no commission in one of the other listings, but the most straightforward and correct choice is D.

34. D. The only thing you know for certain is the nature of the contract, because the broker would be paid in either listing agreement if he were the procuring cause.

35. A. This is a perfect description of a net listing, with the broker keeping as his fee the difference between the net to the owner and the selling price.

36. D. A cooperating broker may represent any of the choices.

37. B. The confusing choice here would have been cooperating broker, because she could be either a buyer's or seller's agent.

38. A. Although any of the incorrect answers may be true sometimes, the salesperson is always considered an employee of the broker for purposes of supervision.

39. B. The multiple listing services are marketing tools to share listings.

40. C. A special agent is hired to perform a limited scope of services, like one real estate transaction.

41. A. Choices B and C are not types of listings, and she will pay in the Choice D agreement even if she sells the house herself.

42. D. This can be taken care of by obtaining the consent of both the buyer and the seller to act as a dual agent.

43. D. This is a tricky question because all of these types of agencies must be in writing even if the written agreement comes after the fact.

44. B. The terms have been clearly stated, so it is express. Only one party, the seller, has agreed to act only if the broker finds a buyer, so it's unilateral.

45. D. The three-day clock for depositing the check starts when the offer is accepted.

46. C. The highest and best use is that use the property can be put to that will result in its highest value.

47. A. Change is a principle of value, not a characteristic of value. The fourth characteristic of value is scarcity.

48. D. Two or more properties when combined may benefit from the increase in size, which allows more varied uses. This increase in value is called plottage.

49. B. Adjusting comparables to the subject is the process of accounting for differences between properties. Reconciling comes near the end of the appraisal process. *Equalization* is a term associated with tax assessment.. Estimating value is the definition of appraising.

50. A. *Functional obsolescence* refers to design flaws or outmoded design features. The gas station is external obsolescence. Painting is physical deterioration. Being close but not next to the train station is probably a positive factor.

51. C. A vacancy and collection loss factor is subtracted from potential gross income to arrive at effective gross income. Operating expenses are subtracted from effective gross income. Debt service is never considered in preparing an operating statement for appraisal purposes.

52. B. In theory, all four of these dates may be the same, but if they are different, the effective date is the date upon which the appraiser's estimate of value is based.

53. A. The economic age life method is also called the straight line method. The breakdown and market extraction methods are more detailed techniques for estimating depreciation. The index method is actually a way to estimate building cost not depreciation.

54. D. The capitalization rate is often referred to as the rate of return. The other three terms are used in income approach appraisals but do not refer to the capitalization rate.

55. B. This question might be tricky because all of the wrong answers might be correct to some extent. But interim use is the best choice because the parking lot is probably only a temporary use that the land is being put to while awaiting development of its highest and best use, an office building.

56. D. The cost approach is useful for special-purpose buildings. The income capitalization approach would be used for large-scale income properties like retail malls and office buildings. The gross rent multiplier approach is best used as the income approach for one- and two-family houses.

57. B. The appraiser reconciles the three values by analyzing them and weighting them according to the type of property being appraised and the method used.

58. C. Potential gross income includes an estimate of market rent plus income from other sources like laundry machines and parking.

59. A. The cost approach is the only valuation approach that estimates land and building separately with a depreciated building value being added to the land value for a total value estimate.

60. B. *Ad valorem* relates to assessed value, which the value property taxes are usually based on.

61. D. The Uniform Standards for Professional Appraisal Practice make it unethical to base an appraisal fee on the value of the property being appraised.

62. D. The other choices are principles of value, but contribution deals with the value or cost of a particular improvement, like a new bathroom, as it affects the overall value of the property.

63. A. Rising interest rates will mean that the amount of money the buyer has available for a mortgage will not go as far as it will when interest rates are lower.

64. A. Using other people's (borrowed) money to extend the buying power of your own money is called leveraging.

65. C. A point is 1% of the amount borrowed.

$275,000 – $60,000 = $215,000 (mortgage amount)

$215,000 × 0.01 = $2,150

66. C. Although choices A and B may also have some effect on the amount of money available, adjusting the discount rate will ultimately directly affect the rates charged for consumer borrowing. The Federal Reserve System does not make direct consumer loans so Choice D is wrong.

67. B. The Federal Deposit Insurance Corporation (FDIC) took over this responsibility after passage of the FIRREA in 1989.

68. D. All the choices relate to financing and mortgage loans, but the definition in the question is the exact definition of equity.

69. C. Choices A, B, and D all relate to the document using the property as security for the note but not the terms of the note itself.

70. B. Amortization results in the loan being paid off gradually over time.

71. A. A negotiable instrument allows a debt to be transferred from one creditor to another.

72. A. Interest on a mortgage loan is calculated this way:

Total Amount Borrowed × Interest Rate

$280,000 × 0.07 = $19,600

73. D. The statute in the California Code only covers the original loan used to purchase the house.

74. C. The percent quoted as the loan-to-value (LTV) ratio is the amount the bank will lend. The remainder is what is needed for the down payment.

100% (purchase price) – 80% LTV = 20% down payment

$330,000 (purchase price) × 0.20 (down payment) = $66,000 (cash needed)

75. A. Discount points raise the yield to the lender above that of the stated interest rate, so if points were paid to secure a 6% loan, the yield to the bank would be more than 6%. How much more depends on how many points are paid.

76. B. Although, at the moment of sale, if the sale price equals the value, choices A and D would be correct, the most accurate choice is B.

77. C. Regulation Z, also known as the Truth in Lending Act, deals with what information must appear in real estate loan advertising.

78. C. This is definitional and the other answer choices are made up.

79. D. Direct loans may be made in other parts of the country where mortgage money may not be readily available, but not in California.

80. D. The graduated-payment mortgage loan has lower payments in the early years of the loan, which do not cover the full payment of principal and interest, thereby adding unpaid charges to the loan amount.

81. D. Choices A, B, and C are different names for the same purchase finance arrangement.

82. C. This is definitional.

83. B. Profit is calculated by multiplying the rate of appreciation by the total price of the house.

$300,000 × 0.25 = $75,000

84. A. The person who makes a will (testator) and dies testate (with a will) has no need for the laws that deal with the inheritance when someone dies without a will (intestate).

85. B. Accession is adding to property by various means including accretion.

86. D. This type of property conveyance, usually done as part of a project like a subdivision, is called a statutory dedication.

87. B. The person conveying the property (the grantor) must sign the deed.

88. D. Title insurance passes on the liability of the grantor to a title insurance company.

89. C. Escrow is created when a binding contract is signed and conditional delivery of documents is agreed to.

90. D. The escrow agent does not provide advice on the merits of the transaction.

91. A. Although the other answers may be descriptive, the proper term is *proration*.

92. B. Because the sellers prepaid this item but will only be in the house for 5 months (note November 1 not November 30), the buyer will owe the seller 7 months' worth of taxes.

$2,400 ÷ 12 months = $200 per month

$200 per month × 7 months = $1,400

93. D. Cloud on title signifies a problem often rendering the title less than marketable.

94. C. Zoning changes are not covered by either policy.

95. B. The term *ad valorem* means "related to the value." Property taxes are calculated on the basis of property value.

96. B. The statutory property tax rate is 1%.

$55,000 × 0.01 = $550

97. A. This is definitional.

98. C. An immediately negotiable check is arguably the easiest to collect on, so it provides the greatest security to the seller.

99. C. The purpose of the Unruh Act was to extend protection from discrimination by business establishments.

100. A. This is definitional.

101. B. Blind ads are illegal.

102. C. The law says 48 hours.

103. C. This is statutory.

104. C. A broker has the same supervisory responsibility regardless of the employment status of the salesperson.

105. A. Commissions are paid to the broker, who then shares the agreed-to amount with the salesperson.

106. C. The three other answers are activities that require a real estate license.

107. A. Choice D is the group that advises the Commissioner of Real Estate.

108. D. Jail would not be a penalty unless some crime were committed beyond violation of the Real Estate Law.

109. D. The 150-day license will not be turned into a regular license unless the child support obligation is satisfied.

110. D. A real estate brokerage corporation must have a corporation license.

111. B. This is statutory.

112. D. Choices A and B require membership in those private organizations, and such membership is not mandatory. The state has no official code of ethics for real estate licensees.

113. C. Both state law and the NAR ethics code require informed consent.

114. A. This is statutory.

115. B. This is statutory.

116. B. Realtor is a trademarked name that comes with voluntary membership by brokers and salespersons in the National Association of Realtors. Although not all real estate licensees are members of NAR, all salespersons must work under the supervision of a broker. Therefore, Choice B is the correct response.

117. B. This is statutory.

118. D. This is statutory.

119. D. This is a matter of statutory tax laws.

120. D. This is statutory. Choice A is made up, Choice B is the closing statement form, and Choice C is made up but hints at the FNMA Appraisal Report Form.

121. A. This is statutory.

122. C. This is statutory.

123. D. This is statutory.

124. D. This is statutory.

125. A. The quality of the school district would most likely be considered an opinion. The other statements, given the fact that they are factually wrong, would more than likely be considered fraudulent misrepresentation.

126. D. These are all situations in which the broker would have to disclose his interest to the buyer.

127. C. Realtor is a trademarked name for members of the National Association of Realtors.

128. A. This is statutory.

129. C. No mention of racial or other protected class issues can be made or considered as value-related.

130. A. The cutoff date for lead-paint disclosure is for houses built before 1978.

131. B. These are high fire hazard areas and must be disclosed to the buyer.

132. D. Don't be confused by the spelling. *Ordnance* refers to military weapons. *Ordinance* refers to public rules and regulations.

133. A. The fact that it is in writing makes this an express contract, and both parties having agreed to act makes this a bilateral agreement.

134. B. The contract is not valid and, therefore, is void because the object of the contract—that is, burning down the building—is illegal.

135. B. Because it's a real estate agreement, it will be in writing, therefore express, and only one party must act, so it is unilateral.

136. D. Listing agreements for rentals of leases for less than a month need not be in writing.

137. D. A common misconception is that the broker always represents the seller. Buyer agency agreements are becoming more common, so the broker may represent the buyer and, in the case of dual agency, the buyer and the seller.

138. C. *Mutual consent* is another term for meeting of the minds.

139. B. At the point at which the buyer's offer was rejected and a counteroffer made, the seller became the offeror and the buyer the offeree.

140. D. A married person is considered an adult for contractual purposes.

141. C. The consideration is paid to obtain the right to purchase property at some future date. It is not refundable.

142. D. The agent's promise to market the property and the seller's promise to compensate the agent are generally expressed in writing.

143. A. This is definitional.

144. B. This is definitional.

145. D. Acceptance of rent and/or negotiating an agreement can change a tenancy at will or tenancy at sufferance into a periodic tenancy.

146. B. Choice A might be confusing, but it's the broker who has to be licensed because the listing agreement is with him.

147. A. Unless there are special prior instructions from the seller, the broker must present all offers.

148. D. This is statutory.

149. D. This is the definition of usury.

150. A. The other documents mentioned might be part of a mortgage application, but the question deals with payment documents.

Answer Sheet for Practice Test 2

(Remove This Sheet and Use It to Mark Your Answers)

CUT HERE

1 Ⓐ Ⓑ Ⓒ Ⓓ	21 Ⓐ Ⓑ Ⓒ Ⓓ	41 Ⓐ Ⓑ Ⓒ Ⓓ	61 Ⓐ Ⓑ Ⓒ Ⓓ
2 Ⓐ Ⓑ Ⓒ Ⓓ	22 Ⓐ Ⓑ Ⓒ Ⓓ	42 Ⓐ Ⓑ Ⓒ Ⓓ	62 Ⓐ Ⓑ Ⓒ Ⓓ
3 Ⓐ Ⓑ Ⓒ Ⓓ	23 Ⓐ Ⓑ Ⓒ Ⓓ	43 Ⓐ Ⓑ Ⓒ Ⓓ	63 Ⓐ Ⓑ Ⓒ Ⓓ
4 Ⓐ Ⓑ Ⓒ Ⓓ	24 Ⓐ Ⓑ Ⓒ Ⓓ	44 Ⓐ Ⓑ Ⓒ Ⓓ	64 Ⓐ Ⓑ Ⓒ Ⓓ
5 Ⓐ Ⓑ Ⓒ Ⓓ	25 Ⓐ Ⓑ Ⓒ Ⓓ	45 Ⓐ Ⓑ Ⓒ Ⓓ	65 Ⓐ Ⓑ Ⓒ Ⓓ
6 Ⓐ Ⓑ Ⓒ Ⓓ	26 Ⓐ Ⓑ Ⓒ Ⓓ	46 Ⓐ Ⓑ Ⓒ Ⓓ	66 Ⓐ Ⓑ Ⓒ Ⓓ
7 Ⓐ Ⓑ Ⓒ Ⓓ	27 Ⓐ Ⓑ Ⓒ Ⓓ	47 Ⓐ Ⓑ Ⓒ Ⓓ	67 Ⓐ Ⓑ Ⓒ Ⓓ
8 Ⓐ Ⓑ Ⓒ Ⓓ	28 Ⓐ Ⓑ Ⓒ Ⓓ	48 Ⓐ Ⓑ Ⓒ Ⓓ	68 Ⓐ Ⓑ Ⓒ Ⓓ
9 Ⓐ Ⓑ Ⓒ Ⓓ	29 Ⓐ Ⓑ Ⓒ Ⓓ	49 Ⓐ Ⓑ Ⓒ Ⓓ	69 Ⓐ Ⓑ Ⓒ Ⓓ
10 Ⓐ Ⓑ Ⓒ Ⓓ	30 Ⓐ Ⓑ Ⓒ Ⓓ	50 Ⓐ Ⓑ Ⓒ Ⓓ	70 Ⓐ Ⓑ Ⓒ Ⓓ
11 Ⓐ Ⓑ Ⓒ Ⓓ	31 Ⓐ Ⓑ Ⓒ Ⓓ	51 Ⓐ Ⓑ Ⓒ Ⓓ	71 Ⓐ Ⓑ Ⓒ Ⓓ
12 Ⓐ Ⓑ Ⓒ Ⓓ	32 Ⓐ Ⓑ Ⓒ Ⓓ	52 Ⓐ Ⓑ Ⓒ Ⓓ	72 Ⓐ Ⓑ Ⓒ Ⓓ
13 Ⓐ Ⓑ Ⓒ Ⓓ	33 Ⓐ Ⓑ Ⓒ Ⓓ	53 Ⓐ Ⓑ Ⓒ Ⓓ	73 Ⓐ Ⓑ Ⓒ Ⓓ
14 Ⓐ Ⓑ Ⓒ Ⓓ	34 Ⓐ Ⓑ Ⓒ Ⓓ	54 Ⓐ Ⓑ Ⓒ Ⓓ	74 Ⓐ Ⓑ Ⓒ Ⓓ
15 Ⓐ Ⓑ Ⓒ Ⓓ	35 Ⓐ Ⓑ Ⓒ Ⓓ	55 Ⓐ Ⓑ Ⓒ Ⓓ	75 Ⓐ Ⓑ Ⓒ Ⓓ
16 Ⓐ Ⓑ Ⓒ Ⓓ	36 Ⓐ Ⓑ Ⓒ Ⓓ	56 Ⓐ Ⓑ Ⓒ Ⓓ	76 Ⓐ Ⓑ Ⓒ Ⓓ
17 Ⓐ Ⓑ Ⓒ Ⓓ	37 Ⓐ Ⓑ Ⓒ Ⓓ	57 Ⓐ Ⓑ Ⓒ Ⓓ	77 Ⓐ Ⓑ Ⓒ Ⓓ
18 Ⓐ Ⓑ Ⓒ Ⓓ	38 Ⓐ Ⓑ Ⓒ Ⓓ	58 Ⓐ Ⓑ Ⓒ Ⓓ	78 Ⓐ Ⓑ Ⓒ Ⓓ
19 Ⓐ Ⓑ Ⓒ Ⓓ	39 Ⓐ Ⓑ Ⓒ Ⓓ	59 Ⓐ Ⓑ Ⓒ Ⓓ	79 Ⓐ Ⓑ Ⓒ Ⓓ
20 Ⓐ Ⓑ Ⓒ Ⓓ	40 Ⓐ Ⓑ Ⓒ Ⓓ	60 Ⓐ Ⓑ Ⓒ Ⓓ	80 Ⓐ Ⓑ Ⓒ Ⓓ

81 Ⓐ Ⓑ Ⓒ Ⓓ	101 Ⓐ Ⓑ Ⓒ Ⓓ	121 Ⓐ Ⓑ Ⓒ Ⓓ	141 Ⓐ Ⓑ Ⓒ Ⓓ
82 Ⓐ Ⓑ Ⓒ Ⓓ	102 Ⓐ Ⓑ Ⓒ Ⓓ	122 Ⓐ Ⓑ Ⓒ Ⓓ	142 Ⓐ Ⓑ Ⓒ Ⓓ
83 Ⓐ Ⓑ Ⓒ Ⓓ	103 Ⓐ Ⓑ Ⓒ Ⓓ	123 Ⓐ Ⓑ Ⓒ Ⓓ	143 Ⓐ Ⓑ Ⓒ Ⓓ
84 Ⓐ Ⓑ Ⓒ Ⓓ	104 Ⓐ Ⓑ Ⓒ Ⓓ	124 Ⓐ Ⓑ Ⓒ Ⓓ	144 Ⓐ Ⓑ Ⓒ Ⓓ
85 Ⓐ Ⓑ Ⓒ Ⓓ	105 Ⓐ Ⓑ Ⓒ Ⓓ	125 Ⓐ Ⓑ Ⓒ Ⓓ	145 Ⓐ Ⓑ Ⓒ Ⓓ
86 Ⓐ Ⓑ Ⓒ Ⓓ	106 Ⓐ Ⓑ Ⓒ Ⓓ	126 Ⓐ Ⓑ Ⓒ Ⓓ	146 Ⓐ Ⓑ Ⓒ Ⓓ
87 Ⓐ Ⓑ Ⓒ Ⓓ	107 Ⓐ Ⓑ Ⓒ Ⓓ	127 Ⓐ Ⓑ Ⓒ Ⓓ	147 Ⓐ Ⓑ Ⓒ Ⓓ
88 Ⓐ Ⓑ Ⓒ Ⓓ	108 Ⓐ Ⓑ Ⓒ Ⓓ	128 Ⓐ Ⓑ Ⓒ Ⓓ	148 Ⓐ Ⓑ Ⓒ Ⓓ
89 Ⓐ Ⓑ Ⓒ Ⓓ	109 Ⓐ Ⓑ Ⓒ Ⓓ	129 Ⓐ Ⓑ Ⓒ Ⓓ	149 Ⓐ Ⓑ Ⓒ Ⓓ
90 Ⓐ Ⓑ Ⓒ Ⓓ	110 Ⓐ Ⓑ Ⓒ Ⓓ	130 Ⓐ Ⓑ Ⓒ Ⓓ	150 Ⓐ Ⓑ Ⓒ Ⓓ
91 Ⓐ Ⓑ Ⓒ Ⓓ	111 Ⓐ Ⓑ Ⓒ Ⓓ	131 Ⓐ Ⓑ Ⓒ Ⓓ	
92 Ⓐ Ⓑ Ⓒ Ⓓ	112 Ⓐ Ⓑ Ⓒ Ⓓ	132 Ⓐ Ⓑ Ⓒ Ⓓ	
93 Ⓐ Ⓑ Ⓒ Ⓓ	113 Ⓐ Ⓑ Ⓒ Ⓓ	133 Ⓐ Ⓑ Ⓒ Ⓓ	
94 Ⓐ Ⓑ Ⓒ Ⓓ	114 Ⓐ Ⓑ Ⓒ Ⓓ	134 Ⓐ Ⓑ Ⓒ Ⓓ	
95 Ⓐ Ⓑ Ⓒ Ⓓ	115 Ⓐ Ⓑ Ⓒ Ⓓ	135 Ⓐ Ⓑ Ⓒ Ⓓ	
96 Ⓐ Ⓑ Ⓒ Ⓓ	116 Ⓐ Ⓑ Ⓒ Ⓓ	136 Ⓐ Ⓑ Ⓒ Ⓓ	
97 Ⓐ Ⓑ Ⓒ Ⓓ	117 Ⓐ Ⓑ Ⓒ Ⓓ	137 Ⓐ Ⓑ Ⓒ Ⓓ	
98 Ⓐ Ⓑ Ⓒ Ⓓ	118 Ⓐ Ⓑ Ⓒ Ⓓ	138 Ⓐ Ⓑ Ⓒ Ⓓ	
99 Ⓐ Ⓑ Ⓒ Ⓓ	119 Ⓐ Ⓑ Ⓒ Ⓓ	139 Ⓐ Ⓑ Ⓒ Ⓓ	
100 Ⓐ Ⓑ Ⓒ Ⓓ	120 Ⓐ Ⓑ Ⓒ Ⓓ	140 Ⓐ Ⓑ Ⓒ Ⓓ	

Directions: For each of the following questions, select the choice that best answers the question.

1. Owner A sells a piece of his property to Buyer B. In order for Owner A to get access to the county road he needs an easement across Buyer B's property. In order to accomplish this, which of the following has to occur?

   A. Owner A must grant an easement appurtenant to Buyer B.
   B. Owner A must grant an easement in gross to Buyer B.
   C. Owner A must reserve an easement in gross for himself.
   D. Owner A must reserve an easement appurtenant for himself.

2. The most serious consequence of the difference between a covenant and a condition in a deed is that

   A. an injunction could be filed to stop a covenant violation.
   B. monetary damages may be awarded for violation of a covenant.
   C. violation of a condition could result in forfeiture of the land.
   D. violation of a covenant could result in forfeiture of the land.

3. A deed restriction was placed on all the properties in a subdivision prohibiting aluminum siding because of its appearance. New vinyl siding has a much more natural appearance and several owners want to use it to re-side their homes. What's the best way to change the restriction?

   A. The people who want to use the vinyl siding should file a lawsuit.
   B. All the homeowners in the subdivision should sign a voluntary agreement.
   C. The people who want to use the vinyl siding should appeal to the local government for a variance.
   D. The restriction cannot be removed.

4. What is the study of population characteristics called?

   A. demography
   B. anthropology
   C. sociology
   D. urban planning

5. Real property includes only

   A. the land.

   B. the land and structures.

   C. the land, structures, and fixtures.

   D. the land, structures, fixtures, and personal property.

6. What is the best term to describe a situation where a person buying a property may not use the property for the manufacture of alcoholic beverages or else title will revert back to the seller?

   A. fee simple condition subsequent

   B. fee simple absolute

   C. fee simple condition precedent

   D. fee simple

7. In his will, Owner A leaves his house to his children subject to a life estate to his sister. The interest held by his children is best described as

   A. fee simple interest.

   B. remainder interest.

   C. reversionary interest.

   D. life interest.

8. Several people concurrently own a piece of property. They may not own the property as

   A. tenants in severalty.

   B. tenants in common.

   C. joint tenants.

   D. tenants in partnership.

9. Which of the following best describes a trust as a form of property ownership?

   A. Title is passed from the trustee to the trustor.

   B. Title is passed from the trustor to the beneficiary.

   C. Title is held by the beneficiary.

   D. Title is held by the trustee on behalf of the beneficiary.

10. In order to benefit from the homestead exclusion, how long does the homeowner have to reinvest the protected equity from the sale of the home?

   A. three months

   B. six months

   C. one year

   D. two years

11. What is the most common type of voluntary lien?

    A. mechanic's lien

    B. tax lien

    C. judgment lien

    D. mortgage lien

12. Owner A owns a piece of property. She subdivides it and sells a landlocked piece of it to Owner B. In order for Owner B to gain access to a nearby road, Owner B seeks an

    A. easement in gross.

    B. easement by eminent domain.

    C. easement by necessity.

    D. easement by reservation.

13. Owner A is selling the northwest quarter of a section of land he owns. How much land is he selling?

    A. 40 acres

    B. 160 acres

    C. 320 acres

    D. 640 acres

14. Lumber is delivered to a house to build a deck. At what point, if any, does the lumber become a fixture?

    A. when it is delivered

    B. when the building permit for the deck is issued

    C. when the deck is complete

    D. none of the above (It never becomes a fixture.)

15. Which unity is common to both joint tenants and tenants in common?

    A. possession

    B. time

    C. title

    D. interest

16. The use of the term *correlative* most closely relates to

    A. littoral rights.

    B. riparian rights.

    C. underground water rights.

    D. rights of appropriation.

GO ON TO THE NEXT PAGE

Practice Test 2

17. A surveyor you hire mentions terms like *baselines* and *meridians* when surveying your property. What system of legal description is he most likely using?

A. government survey
B. metes and bounds
C. Spanish land grant
D. lot and block

18. A, B, and C own property as joint tenants. A sells her share to D. What is the new status of the ownership?

A. B, C, and D are now all joint tenants.
B. B, C, and D are now all tenants in common.
C. B and C are tenants in common and D is a joint tenant.
D. B and C are joint tenants with each other and D is a tenant in common with them.

19. Which of the following will not cause a cloud on the title to real estate?

A. mechanic's lien
B. pending eminent domain action
C. pending action for adverse possession
D. pending zoning change

20. Owner A gives the county a subsurface easement across her property to build a sewer line. This is best described as an

A. easement appurtenant by grant.
B. easement in gross by grant.
C. easement appurtenant by condemnation.
D. easement in gross by condemnation.

21. Merger of the servient tenement with the dominant tenement best describes

A. the creation of an easement.
B. a landlord-tenant relationship.
C. the termination of an easement.
D. the creation of a license.

22. The smallest subdivision affected by the Subdivision Map Act is a subdivision comprising

A. two or more parcels.
B. five or more parcels.
C. five or more parcels if none is larger than 160 acres.
D. five or more lots if none is smaller than 160 acres.

23. Under the California Environmental Quality Act of 1970, an environmental impact report must be prepared for

    A. all subdivisions.

    B. all subdivisions that will have a substantial environmental impact.

    C. all subdivisions coming under the Subdivision Map Act.

    D. only large-scale subdivisions.

24. Owner A owns 10 acres on which there is a deed restriction prohibiting subdivision of the land into smaller parcels. The local zoning permits homes to be built on parcels of 2 acres or more. Which of the following is true?

    A. Owner A may subdivide his land.

    B. Owner A may not subdivide his land.

    C. The land may only be subdivided if Owner A sells the property in order to eliminate the deed restriction.

    D. Owner A may subdivide the land but must sell the properties with the same deed restrictions in place.

25. When a home is sold to pay off unpaid debts, the first debt to be paid is

    A. tax liens.

    B. first mortgages lines.

    C. the earliest lien filed by date.

    D. the lien with the largest amount of money due.

26. Neighbor A built a fence 2 feet onto Owner B's property. This is best described as a(n)

    A. easement.

    B. encroachment.

    C. prescriptive right.

    D. adverse possession.

27. Owner A owns a 3-story building on property that is zoned for construction of a 20-story building. Owner A does not want to sell his building but wants to make some additional money from it. Assuming his actions are in accordance with local development codes, what might he do?

    A. Seek a right of correlative use.

    B. Sell his air rights.

    C. Seek a zoning change.

    D. There is nothing he can do to derive additional income from his property.

28. An agent employed to handle a number of different matters on behalf of someone is called a

    A. general agent.

    B. universal agent.

    C. special agent.

    D. unlimited agent.

GO ON TO THE NEXT PAGE

29. Which of the following is a requirement to make an exclusive listing agreement valid?

    A. a description of the marketing plan

    B. a definite termination date

    C. the specified names of the salespersons working on the listing

    D. a statement of the minimum broker expenditures on the listing

30. The state has taken Seller A's property by eminent domain for a highway after she listed it for sale. What happens to the listing agreement?

    A. Nothing.

    B. It is terminated.

    C. It is automatically modified to account for the state purchasing the property.

    D. The commission is modified to account for a lower selling price.

31. A written disclosure of agency representation is required for

    A. all real estate transactions.

    B. all residential transactions.

    C. one- to ten-unit residential transactions.

    D. one- to four-unit residential transactions.

32. An implied agency

    A. is created in writing.

    B. is created orally.

    C. is created by the actions of the parties.

    D. cannot be created.

33. The type of authority specified in an agency agreement is called

    A. fiduciary authority.

    B. actual authority.

    C. implied authority.

    D. apparent authority.

34. Depositing a buyer's deposit check in the broker's business operating account is

    A. acceptable only after the offer has been accepted.

    B. called commingling and is legal any time.

    C. can be done up to the time the offer is accepted.

    D. called commingling and is a violation.

35. Which of the following types of listing agreements do not require the broker to be compensated unless she is the procuring cause?

    A. open listing and multiple listing

    B. exclusive-agency listing and exclusive-right-to-sell listing

    C. net listing and exclusive-right-to-sell listing

    D. open listing and exclusive-agency listing

36. A buyer's agent knows that the buyer is anxious to purchase a house so that he can enroll his children in school before the school year starts. What must the agent do with this information?

    A. Disclose it to the seller as a material fact.

    B. Disclose it to the seller's agent but remind the agent that it must be kept confidential.

    C. Keep the information confidential.

    D. Keep the information confidential unless the agent thinks revealing it will result in a quick closing.

37. The principle of loyalty as a fiduciary requires the agent to put

    A. the principal's interest above all others except the agent's.

    B. the third party's interest above the agent's interest.

    C. the principal's interest above all others.

    D. all the agent's and subagent's interests before all others including his own.

38. Broker A has a listing to sell Seller B's property. Broker A shows the property to his cousin, who is interested in the property. What problem can potentially arise?

    A. none

    B. undisclosed dual agency, unless Broker A reveals the relationship to Seller B and Seller B is okay with it

    C. none, as long as Broker A gets his cousin to sign a buyer's agency agreement

    D. none, as long as Broker A doesn't represent his cousin as a buyer's agent

39. In what type of listing might the broker be both principal and agent?

    A. multiple listing

    B. option listing

    C. open listing

    D. none, because doing so would be illegal

40. Under the duty of obedience, which of the following requests from the seller should the agent not obey?

    A. The seller tells the agent to bring buyers who have been financially qualified by a bank.

    B. The seller tells the agent not to show the house when the seller is not home.

    C. The seller tells the agent to only show houses to minority families.

    D. The seller tells the agent not to tell any of the neighbors the house is for sale.

GO ON TO THE NEXT PAGE

Practice Test 2

41. Broker A has an exclusive authorization and right-to-sell listing agreement to sell Seller B's house for $300,000. Broker A brings Buyer C to see the house. Buyer C immediately makes a full cash offer of $300,000 to buy the house with no contingencies in the contract. Seller B decides he can probably get more for the house and refuses the offer, raising the asking price of the house. Does Seller B owe the broker a commission?

    A. Yes, because Broker A produced a buyer who met all of Seller B's terms.

    B. No, because the house didn't actually sell.

    C. Yes, but only if the house sells at the new price.

    D. No, because Seller B was not a ready, willing, and able seller.

42. Buyer A hires Broker B as a buyer's broker. Broker B assures Buyer A that her fee will be paid for by the seller. To whom does Broker B owe his fiduciary duty in this arrangement?

    A. Buyer A, because she is the principal

    B. the seller, because he is paying Broker B's fee

    C. no one, because this is a dual-agency situation

    D. the cooperating broker who represents the seller, because Broker B becomes a subagent

43. Five years ago, Seller A added a deck onto her house but never got a building permit for it. What obligation, if any, does Seller A have with respect to the deck when she decides to sell her house?

    A. She has no obligation, because the five-year statutory limit has elapsed.

    B. She must advise the real estate agent who can advise her as to what to do.

    C. She must secure the proper permit before selling the house.

    D. She must advise the buyer of the situation.

44. Broker A is hired as a buyer's broker to help Buyer B find a house. Broker A is considered a

    A. universal agent.

    B. special agent.

    C. general agent.

    D. designated agent.

45. Seller A tells Broker B, who is representing her in the sale of her house, not to disclose the fact that the house has a leaky roof. Broker B agrees and does not reveal the information to the buyer. Which of the following statements is true?

    A. This is not a problem because the buyer should have discovered the situation through due diligence.

    B. Only Seller A is liable, because he issued the orders.

    C. Only Broker B is liable, because he has a duty of honesty to the buyer.

    D. Both Seller A and Broker B are liable.

46. The market value of a property is its

    A. highest price.
    B. average price.
    C. most probable price.
    D. sales price.

47. In order for a use to be considered the highest and best use of a property, it must be physically possible as well as

    A. legally permissible.
    B. financially feasible.
    C. maximally productive.
    D. all of the above

48. The most reliable method for appraising single-family homes is the

    A. cost approach.
    B. sales comparison approach.
    C. gross rent multiplier approach.
    D. income capitalization approach.

49. In the sales comparison approach, a condition of sale adjustment would be made for a property that had been subject to

    A. weather damage.
    B. fire.
    C. foreclosure.
    D. below-market financing.

50. The positive effect on value that larger homes have on a smaller home in the neighborhood is known as

    A. conformity.
    B. anticipation.
    C. change.
    D. progression.

51. You spent $10,000 to remodel your bathroom and found that it only added $5,000 to the overall value of your house. This is an example of what economic principle?

    A. contribution
    B. change
    C. anticipation
    D. conformity

Practice Test 2

GO ON TO THE NEXT PAGE

52. Total depreciation from all sources is a good definition of

    A. physical deterioration.
    B. accrued depreciation.
    C. functional obsolescence.
    D. age life depreciation.

53. According to federal regulations, a licensed or certified appraiser is required for all federally related transaction appraisals for properties valued above

    A. $50,000
    B. $100,000
    C. $200,000
    D. $250,000

54. Which of the following is not representative of a market-value transaction?

    A. There is special financing.
    B. The buyer and seller are related.
    C. The buyer but not the seller knows the property is being rezoned.
    D. all of the above

55. In the cost approach to valuation, the cost to create an exact duplicate of the building is called its

    A. replacement cost.
    B. depreciated cost.
    C. rebuilding cost.
    D. reproduction cost.

56. In the sales comparison approach, adjustments are made to

    A. the subject to make it like the comparable.
    B. the comparable to make it like the subject.
    C. one comparable to make it like another comparable.
    D. both the subject and the comparable.

57. Using the gross rent multiplier method, what is the value of a residential property improved with a four-unit building where each unit rents for $750 per month and the typical multiplier is 157?

    A. $491,000
    B. $391,000
    C. $241,300
    D. $117,000

58. "The value of a property is determined by the cost to purchase a property of similar usefulness" is a good definition of the principle of

   A. progression.
   B. change.
   C. highest and best use.
   D. substitution.

59. In the cost approach, accrued depreciation is

   A. added to the reproduction or replacement cost.
   B. deducted from the replacement or reproduction cost.
   C. only based on physical deterioration.
   D. only calculated if the structure is more than ten years old.

60. A subject property has four bedrooms. The comparable property has three bedrooms and recently sold for $225,000. The value of a bedroom is estimated to be $30,000. In all other respects, the properties are the same. What is the indicated value of the subject property?

   A. $195,000
   B. $225,000
   C. $255,000
   D. Not enough information is provided.

61. An extremely contemporary house in a neighborhood of colonial homes might suffer a negative influence on its value because it violates the principle of

   A. anticipation.
   B. change.
   C. competition.
   D. conformity.

62. When considering depreciation, the concept of whether an item of physical deterioration is curable or incurable is a function

   A. only of its cost.
   B. only of the value it adds.
   C. of whether the item can actually be corrected.
   D. of its cost relative to the value it adds.

63. If the reproduction cost of a house is $300,000 with an economic life of 50 years, how much does the house depreciate each year using the straight line method of calculating depreciation?

   A. $10,000
   B. $6,000
   C. $5,000
   D. $2,000

Practice Test 2

GO ON TO THE NEXT PAGE

64. Buyer A borrows money to buy a house. As part of the repayment plan, when he sells the house he will have to turn over a portion of the profit he makes on the house to the lender. This type of mortgage is called a

    A. shared appreciation mortgage.

    B. graduated payment mortgage.

    C. reverse annuity mortgage.

    D. growing equity mortgage.

65. The difference between the primary mortgage market and the secondary mortgage market is that the secondary market

    A. only lends money to member banks.

    B. buys mortgages from primary lenders.

    C. provides guarantees to lenders for borrowers who would otherwise be unqualified to buy property.

    D. subsidizes primary lenders by using creative financing.

66. A mortgage loan that results in the entire principal balance being due at the end of the term after all other payments have been made is referred to as a(n)

    A. negative amortization loan.

    B. fully amortized loan.

    C. interest-only loan.

    D. partially amortized loan.

67. What is the loan-to-value ratio above which a borrower will typically have to purchase private mortgage insurance?

    A. 100%

    B. 95%

    C. 90%

    D. 80%

68. A conforming loan is defined as one

    A. for an amount that meets Federal National Mortgage Association (FNMA) standards.

    B. for a house in a neighborhood of conforming properties.

    C. that is protected by private mortgage insurance (PMI).

    D. that is fully amortized.

69. The potential benefits of a sale leaseback arrangement include all of the following except

    A. freeing up cash for the original owner.

    B. liquidity of the investment.

    C. being able to deduct depreciation on the building.

    D. deductibility of lease payments.

70. Which of the following pairs consists of terms meaning essentially the same thing?

   A. trustor and lender
   B. mortgagor and lender
   C. foreclosure and trustee's sale
   D. mortgagee and borrower

71. Which of the following would not be considered an institutional lender?

   A. credit union
   B. insurance company
   C. commercial bank
   D. mortgage company

72. Maximum loan broker commissions are set by

   A. individual brokers because all commissions are negotiable.
   B. Regulation Z.
   C. the Truth in Lending Law.
   D. the Real Property Loan Law.

73. A purchaser of a $200,000 home using Federal Housing Administration (FHA) financing would have to make a minimum cash investment of

   A. $2,000.
   B. $4,000.
   C. $6,000.
   D. $10,000.

74. Buyer A is purchasing a home for $375,000 and is getting a mortgage loan at a loan-to-value ratio of 80%. The lender is charging 2 points to secure a lower interest rate. How much will the borrower have to pay in points?

   A. $3,750
   B. $6,000
   C. $7,500
   D. $75,000

75. The best description of a holder in due course is

   A. a note purchaser.
   B. a note maker.
   C. the original note holder.
   D. the original borrower.

GO ON TO THE NEXT PAGE

76. The right of redemption exists in the case of

    A. a judicial foreclosure.

    B. a trustee's sale.

    C. neither A nor B

    D. both A and B

77. The court order to evict the former owner of a home that has been sold through a trustee's sale is called

    A. unlawful detainer.

    B. judicial foreclosure.

    C. deficiency judgment.

    D. notice of default.

78. Protection extended to homeowners to avoid losing their homes as a result of an installment purchase of goods or services was created by

    A. the Real Estate Settlement Procedures Act (RESPA).

    B. the Unruh Act.

    C. Regulation Z.

    D. the Equal Credit Opportunity Act (ECOA).

79. In a deed of trust situation, who can claim the property in the event of a default of payments on the mortgage loan?

    A. trustee

    B. trustor

    C. beneficiary

    D. mortgagor

80. Which of the following do not make direct mortgage loans?

    A. insurance companies

    B. mortgage bankers

    C. commercial banks

    D. mortgage brokers

81. What is the first month's interest on an amortized 30-year loan for $250,000 at 7% interest?

    A. $17,500

    B. $1,750

    C. $1,458

    D. $583

82. Buyer A closes on a house for which he borrowed $300,000 to purchase. Two days later, he changes his mind about buying the house and wants to use his right to rescind the mortgage. Can he?

- **A.** Yes.
- **B.** No.
- **C.** Yes, but only if he bought the house as an investment.
- **D.** He can only cancel the first (purchase money) mortgage.

83. A mortgage lender provides a borrower with a good-faith estimate of the closing costs and a special booklet that meets HUD requirements. The lender is complying with what law/act?

- **A.** RESPA
- **B.** Truth in Lending Law
- **C.** ECOA
- **D.** Unruh Act

84. A holographic will is valid if it is

- **A.** witnessed by one witness.
- **B.** completely handwritten by the maker of the will (testator/testatrix).
- **C.** recorded in the county recorder's office.
- **D.** witnessed by two witnesses.

85. The product of accretion is known as

- **A.** improvement.
- **B.** alluvium.
- **C.** accession.
- **D.** reliction.

86. The property of a person who dies intestate and with no heirs will be claimed by the state in a process called

- **A.** escheat.
- **B.** succession.
- **C.** devisement.
- **D.** bequeathing.

87. Which of the following in not a requirement for a valid deed?

- **A.** the signature of the grantee
- **B.** a deed in writing
- **C.** a granting clause
- **D.** a description of the property

GO ON TO THE NEXT PAGE

88. The form of deed that carries no warrantees, implied or actual, is a

    A. grant deed.
    B. quitclaim deed.
    C. gift deed.
    D. warranty deed.

89. Escrow instructions given by one party at a time to the escrow agent are called

    A. bilateral.
    B. conditional.
    C. unilateral.
    D. settlement.

90. An escrow agent pays a referral fee to any brokers who send him business. Which of the following is correct?

    A. As long as the referral fees are limited to licensed brokers, he is not breaking the law.
    B. He is violating no law.
    C. He is breaking the law.
    D. There is no violation of the law provided the principals are informed of this practice.

91. Closing of title in escrow is considered complete when

    A. parties agree in writing that escrow is complete.
    B. documents are mailed or delivered to both parties.
    C. funds are disbursed.
    D. documents are recorded.

92. A seller pays the yearly taxes of $3,600 in advance on July 1. He closes on the sale of the house on November 15. Who owes what to whom?

    A. The buyer owes the seller $2,260.
    B. The seller owes the buyer $2,260.
    C. The buyer owes the seller $1,340.
    D. The seller owes the buyer $1,340.

93. Which of the following terms does not belong with the others?

    A. lot books
    B. marketable title
    C. general indexes
    D. title plant

94. Title insurance premiums are paid

  A. by the buyer.
  B. by the seller.
  C. by the lender.
  D. according to local custom and negotiation.

95. What is the annual inflation factor permitted for local property taxes?

  A. 2%
  B. 3%
  C. 4%
  D. 5%

96. An owner-occupied home is entitled to how much of an exemption from the value of the property for tax purposes?

  A. $0
  B. $4,000
  C. $5,000
  D. $7,000

97. An uncashed deposit check may be kept by a broker for

  A. four days after offer acceptance.
  B. five days after offer acceptance.
  C. seven days after offer acceptance.
  D. whatever time period the principal authorizes.

98. An agent wanting to avoid charges of commingling funds might do all of the following except

  A. accept the buyer's offer with no deposit.
  B. have the deposit check made out to the escrow agent.
  C. deposit the check immediately into a separate trust account.
  D. hold the uncashed check in his files for the statutory time period.

99. The primary focus of the 1866 Civil Rights Act was

  A. freeing the slaves.
  B. preventing housing discrimination on the basis of religion.
  C. preventing housing discrimination on the basis of race.
  D. providing fair housing opportunities for European immigrants.

Practice Test 2

GO ON TO THE NEXT PAGE

100. The California Fair Employment and Housing Act was formerly known as the

    A. Rumford Housing Act.

    B. Unruh Civil Rights Act.

    C. Housing Financial Discrimination Act.

    D. California Fair Housing Act.

101. The placement of an ad for the sale of a property through a real estate broker without disclosing that fact in the ad is called

    A. blind advertising and is legal.

    B. disclosable advertising and is legal.

    C. blind advertising and is illegal.

    D. closed advertising and is illegal.

102. In order for a mobile home to be advertised for sale by a broker, it must be in a mobile home park or a location where it can remain

    A. for at least one year.

    B. for at least two years.

    C. for at least three years.

    D. indefinitely.

103. If a transaction does not close, for how long must a broker keep the records?

    A. Records do not have to be maintained if the transaction didn't close.

    B. one year from listing

    C. two years from listing

    D. three years from listing

104. For purposes of the state license law, the relationship between broker and salesperson is always

    A. determined by the type of agreement they have.

    B. that of employer and employee.

    C. that of employer and independent contractor.

    D. determined by how the employment taxes are paid.

105. An unlicensed real estate assistant can be compensated by

    A. the broker.

    B. the salesperson.

    C. the client.

    D. either A or B

106. How many members are on the California Real Estate Advisory Commission (not including the commissioner)?

    A. four
    B. five
    C. eight
    D. ten

107. A restricted license could require a licensee to

    A. only work in a certain area.
    B. only work for a certain broker.
    C. only sell commercial property.
    D. all of the above

108. Which of the following would constitute a real estate license law violation?

    A. commingling client's and broker's funds
    B. neglecting to secure informed seller consent when combining an option with a listing agreement
    C. undisclosed dual agency
    D. all of the above

109. What course must be completed before a candidate for real estate licensure can take the state salesperson's licensing examination?

    A. none
    B. Real Estate Principles
    C. Real Estate Economics
    D. Real Estate Practice

110. Which of the following would not prevent a real estate license from being issued?

    A. conviction of a felony
    B. no Social Security number on the application
    C. the applicant being only 18 years old
    D. failure to reveal a criminal conviction on the application

111. The California Real Estate Recovery Account is funded by

    A. the state income tax.
    B. 5% of local property taxes.
    C. 5% of real estate license fees.
    D. 5% of property transfer fees.

Practice Test 2

GO ON TO THE NEXT PAGE

112. Which of the following is true?

    A. California has adopted its own code of ethics for real estate licensees.

    B. California recommends study and observance of the National Association of Realtors (NAR) code of ethics.

    C. California considers any behavior in the practice of real estate not covered by the law to be strictly optional.

    D. California requires all real estate licensees to be members of some professional association so that they are covered by a code of ethics.

113. According to the NAR code of ethics, once a seller has accepted an offer, a Realtor

    A. does not need to present further offers.

    B. can stop marketing the property.

    C. must wait until closing to collect his commission.

    D. should advise the seller to take a subsequent higher offer.

114. Before taking the state license examination to be a real estate salesperson, a person must have at least completed or be enrolled in a course in

    A. real estate principles.

    B. legal aspects of real estate.

    C. real estate practice.

    D. real estate economics.

115. A real estate broker operating a prepaid rental listing service is exempt from

    A. having a Prepaid Rental Listing Service (PRLS) license.

    B. the security bond requirement.

    C. neither A nor B

    D. both A and B

116. A licensee who has had her license suspended by the real estate commissioner after a hearing may appeal to the

    A. state real estate board.

    B. district attorney.

    C. attorney general.

    D. courts.

117. Antitrust laws prohibit

    A. a broker discussing a commission with a client.

    B. a broker discussing a commission with her employee salesperson.

    C. a broker discussing a commission with a cooperating broker.

    D. a broker discussing a commission with a competing broker.

118. Which of the following agreements must be in writing?

    A. a lease for two years

    B. a lease for one year that is signed today but will begin in four months

    C. a property purchase option agreement

    D. all of the above

119. A material fact and a material defect are the same thing

    A. always.

    B. never.

    C. sometimes.

    D. in every way except as to disclosure requirements.

120. The obligation of a broker or salesperson to inspect a property for physical defects was based on

    A. the Mello-Roos Act.

    B. *Easton v. Strassburger.*

    C. *United States v. Foley.*

    D. *Jones v. Mayer.*

121. Disclosure requirements for a real estate agent are limited to

    A. agency relationships.

    B. dual agency relationships.

    C. material facts.

    D. material facts and all agency relationships.

122. Damage or destruction that occurs to a property before escrow closes but after the purchase contract is signed

    A. is the responsibility of the seller.

    B. is the responsibility of the buyer.

    C. is the responsibility of the holder of equitable title.

    D. would normally be negotiated in the contract.

123. An applicant for a real estate salesperson's license is behind on his child support payments and his name comes up on a delinquent payment list. What type of license can he be issued?

    A. a regular real estate salesperson's license

    B. a provisional 90-day license

    C. a temporary 180-day license

    D. a temporary 150-day license

Practice Test 2

GO ON TO THE NEXT PAGE

124. What is the limit on the cost of work that can be done by an unlicensed contractor?

    A. less than $500

    B. less than $1,000

    C. less than $2,000

    D. less than $2,500

125. The practice of real estate without a real estate license is prosecuted by

    A. the California Real Estate Advisory Commission.

    B. the California attorney general.

    C. the district attorney in the appropriate jurisdiction.

    D. town or city attorneys.

126. A warranty of authority

    A. guarantees the house against physical defects.

    B. guarantees the house against title defects.

    C. insures the principal against the agent's actions.

    D. makes the principal responsible for certain agent actions.

127. Use of the term *Realtor* unless one has the right to use the term

    A. is illegal.

    B. can result in loss of license.

    C. is unethical.

    D. all of the above

128. A real estate salesperson working as an independent contractor will have

    A. payroll taxes taken out of his salary.

    B. health insurance coverage.

    C. Social Security taxes taken out of his salary.

    D. workers' compensation coverage.

129. Special disclosures that must be made by sellers of condominiums and common interest subdivisions include

    A. average income of the owners.

    B. average age of the owners.

    C. minutes of the past 12 months of homeowners' association meetings.

    D. recent physical inspection reports on common facilities.

130. Houses built before what year require a lead-based paint disclosure to buyers?

    A. 1978
    B. 1979
    C. 1980
    D. 1984

131. The Natural Hazards Disclosure Act requires such disclosure for

    A. virtually all properties.
    B. all vacant land.
    C. one-family houses.
    D. one- to four-family houses.

132. Under the appropriate circumstances, all but which of the following disclosures will be required to be provided by a seller?

    A. lead-based paint disclosure
    B. ordnance location disclosure
    C. earthquake fault zone disclosure
    D. demographic change disclosure

133. Owner A discusses the terms of selling his property with Buyer B. They agree on the amount of money, the type of deed, and when the closing will be. This contract for the sale of the property is

    A. valid and enforceable.
    B. void and unenforceable.
    C. valid and voidable.
    D. valid and unenforceable.

134. The major difference between a unilateral and a bilateral contract is that

    A. in a unilateral contract, both people must act; in a bilateral contract only one must act.
    B. in a unilateral contract only one party agrees to do something; in a bilateral contract both agree to do something.
    C. in a unilateral contract, only one party must act; in a bilateral contract, both parties must act.
    D. There is no difference as long as the contract is in writing.

135. Buyer A signs an agreement with Seller B to purchase her home. Seller B changes her mind about selling, but Buyer A still wants the house. Buyer B files a suit for

    A. rescission.
    B. release.
    C. specific performance.
    D. novation.

Practice Test 2

GO ON TO THE NEXT PAGE

136. A homeowner places an advertisement in the newspaper offering her home for sale and offering to compensate any broker who brings a successful buyer to the property. The homeowner is seeking to create an

A. express bilateral option listing.
B. express unilateral open listing.
C. express bilateral exclusive listing.
D. express unilateral exclusive agency listing.

137. Which of the following is most correct about buyer broker compensation?

A. The fee paid by the seller is credited against the fee owed by the buyer.
B. The broker collects a fee from the seller and the buyer.
C. The broker collects a fee from the buyer.
D. The broker collects a fee from the seller.

138. Which of the following is not a requirement of a valid real estate sales contract?

A. acknowledgment
B. consideration
C. offer and acceptance
D. that the contract is in writing

139. A real estate sales contract entered into by an emancipated minor is

A. void.
B. voidable.
C. valid.
D. unenforceable.

140. Farmer A plants 3 acres of his land in tomatoes and then sells his property to Buyer B. If the contract of sale is silent about the tomatoes, who has the right to harvest the crop?

A. the new owner
B. the farmer
C. Both must share the crop equally.
D. The real estate agent will most likely have to settle any dispute.

141. Which of the following is correct regarding the statute of limitations in which to bring an action to enforce written and oral contracts?

A. written, two years; oral, four years
B. written, four years; oral, two years
C. written and oral, two years
D. written and oral, four years

142. A broker acting without a listing agreement must follow whose instructions with respect to the buyer's deposit?

    A. the buyer's

    B. the seller's

    C. neither, by not cashing the check

    D. neither, by turning it over to the seller

143. Landlord A leased an apartment to Tenant B for six months. Landlord A failed to specify when the rent payment was due. When can he expect to get his rent?

    A. at the end of the six months

    B. at the beginning of the six months

    C. at the beginning of each month

    D. at the end of each month

144. A written lease may be changed by all of the following except

    A. oral agreement.

    B. written amendment.

    C. actions of the parties.

    D. novation.

145. A periodic tenancy without a lease for agricultural and grazing land is assumed to run

    A. for one year.

    B. for six months.

    C. month to month.

    D. until the end of the growing season.

146. In addition to the usual elements of a contract, a real property land contract must include

    A. the interest rate being charged.

    B. a list of easements.

    C. the number of years to complete the contract.

    D. an acceleration clause.

147. A lease option for a house

    A. gives the tenant the right to renew the lease.

    B. gives the optionee the right to negotiate to rent the house at some future date.

    C. gives the tenant the right of possession and the right to purchase the house in the future.

    D. commits the tenant to buy the house at a pre-agreed-upon price at some future date.

GO ON TO THE NEXT PAGE

148. Fees charged to a tenant in a mobile home park are limited to all of the following except

   A. occupancy fee.
   B. service charges.
   C. utilities.
   D. rent.

149. The type of note that reduces the bank's risk of changing interest rates is called the

   A. straight note.
   B. term note.
   C. installment note.
   D. adjustable rate note.

150. The last payment on a mortgage loan that is at least twice as much as any other payment and generally is made at the end of the term to pay off the loan is called

   A. an hypothecation.
   B. a term payment.
   C. a balloon payment.
   D. the last payment.

Answer Key for Practice Test 2

1. D	**36.** C	**71.** D
2. C	**37.** C	**72.** D
3. B	**38.** B	**73.** C
4. A	**39.** B	**74.** B
5. C	**40.** C	**75.** A
6. A	**41.** A	**76.** A
7. B	**42.** A	**77.** A
8. A	**43.** D	**78.** B
9. D	**44.** B	**79.** C
10. B	**45.** D	**80.** D
11. D	**46.** C	**81.** C
12. C	**47.** D	**82.** B
13. B	**48.** B	**83.** A
14. C	**49.** C	**84.** B
15. A	**50.** D	**85.** B
16. C	**51.** A	**86.** A
17. A	**52.** B	**87.** A
18. D	**53.** D	**88.** B
19. D	**54.** D	**89.** C
20. B	**55.** D	**90.** C
21. C	**56.** B	**91.** D
22. A	**57.** A	**92.** C
23. B	**58.** D	**93.** B
24. B	**59.** B	**94.** D
25. A	**60.** C	**95.** A
26. B	**61.** D	**96.** D
27. B	**62.** D	**97.** D
28. A	**63.** B	**98.** A
29. B	**64.** A	**99.** C
30. B	**65.** B	**100.** A
31. D	**66.** C	**101.** C
32. C	**67.** D	**102.** A
33. B	**68.** A	**103.** D
34. D	**69.** B	**104.** B
35. D	**70.** C	**105.** D

106. D		**121.** D		**136.** B	
107. D		**122.** A		**137.** A	
108. D		**123.** D		**138.** A	
109. A		**124.** A		**139.** C	
110. C		**125.** C		**140.** A	
111. C		**126.** D		**141.** B	
112. B		**127.** D		**142.** A	
113. B		**128.** D		**143.** A	
114. A		**129.** C		**144.** A	
115. D		**130.** A		**145.** A	
116. D		**131.** A		**146.** C	
117. D		**132.** D		**147.** C	
118. D		**133.** B		**148.** A	
119. C		**134.** C		**149.** D	
120. B		**135.** C		**150.** C	

Answers and Explanations for Practice Test 2

1. **D.** Because this easement attaches itself to Owner A's land, it is an easement appurtenant so choices B and C are incorrect. An owner selling property and needing to retain an easement across the property sold reserves an easement.

2. **C.** Forefeiture of the land is more serious than an injunction or monetary damages so choices A and B are incorrect. Only violation of a condition can result in forfeiture of the property.

3. **B.** Variances do not apply because this is not a government restriction. Court action may be necessary but only if the other owners refuse the change.

4. **A.** This is definitional.

5. **C.** Real property does not include personal property.

6. **A.** The question implies that a stipulation is present in the deed so either Choice A or Choice C might be correct. However, the fact that ownership is taken first but the title may be lost after ownership has passed would indicate that this is a condition subsequent. A condition precedent would be a condition that must be fulfilled before title fully passes to the new owner.

7. **B.** The children have only a partial interest in the property. The possessory interest remains. Therefore, they have a remainder interest.

8. **A.** Tenancy in severalty is ownership by only one person. All the other forms of ownership are for two or more people.

9. **D.** In a trust, title is passed from the trustor to the trustee. The trustee holds the title on behalf of the beneficiary.

10. **B.** The state homestead law requires reinvestment in a new home within six months.

11. **D.** The first three types of liens are put on the property involuntarily. A mortgage lien is voluntary because we agree to the lien in return for the funds we are borrowing.

12. **C.** Where someone has created the situation that requires an easement (subdividing property) an easement by necessity may be granted.

13. **B.** You need to remember that a section contains 640 acres. One-quarter of a section is 0.25×640, or 160 acres.

14. **C.** The lumber is personal property until the deck is built and becomes a part of the real estate.

15. **A.** The other three unities are only features of joint tenancy.

16. **C.** The right of correlative use is the right of a landowner to use water under his property.

17. **A.** These terms are only associated with the government or rectangular survey system.

18. **D.** In the situation described, C and B remain joint tenants but D becomes a tenant in common as to that share.

19. **D.** Choices A, B, and C limit or may limit the ownership of the property. Although zoning may affect profitability or value, it does not affect title to a property.

20. **B.** You have to examine both parts of each answer as it relates to the question. Because this easement does not benefit an adjacent landowner, it is not an easement appurtenant. This eliminates choices A and C. Owner A gave the easement to the county; the county did not take the easement against her will. This eliminates eminent domain (Choice D).

21. **C.** One of the ways easements are terminated is by the joining of the two properties or interests.

22. **A.** The three wrong answer choices relate to the Subdivided Lands Law.

23. **B.** Choice D is too vague and the other answers do not apply.

24. **B.** The rule is that if a deed restriction and local laws conflict, the stricter rule will apply. In this case, the deed restriction is stricter than the local zoning.

25. A. This is known as the priority of liens and, in general, tax liens are always first regardless of date filed.

26. B. This encroachment may eventually become an adverse possession or prescriptive easement situation, but until it does it is an encroachment.

27. B. There are likely a number of things he can do, including tearing down the building and rebuilding; this was not a choice, but it does eliminate Choice D. Choice A relates to water rights, and he already has zoning, which would allow him to build a bigger building.

28. A. This is the definition of a general agent.

29. B. The other answers are not required, but a termination date is.

30. B. An operation of law or destruction of the property (in a sense, either might apply) terminates a listing.

31. D. The law requires this.

32. C. An implied agency is created by the actions of the parties, which are later confirmed in some type of written agreement.

33. B. Fiduciary might be the confusing answer here, but fiduciary relates to the obligations of the agent not his authority.

34. D. Commingling can result in disciplinary action.

35. D. This is definitional for these two types of listings.

36. C. The agent could reveal the information if the buyer authorized him to do so but not on his own authority.

37. C. Loyalty requires that the principal's interest be placed before all other interests including that of the broker.

38. B. The implication here is that it would be difficult for a broker not to represent a family member, thus creating a dual agency.

39. B. The option listing, which is legal, gives the broker the right to buy the property, so the broker could be both principal and agent.

40. C. Obedience is limited to those activities that are legal. Answer C is reverse discrimination and illegal.

41. A. The broker produced a ready, willing, and able buyer who met all the terms and conditions of the seller. The broker earned his commission.

42. A. The broker owes his fiduciary duty to the principal, in this case the buyer, regardless of who pays the fee.

43. D. This is the most correct answer. The agent should be advised and the owner could secure a permit to avoid problems with the sale, but her obligation is to reveal the lack of the permit to the buyer.

44. B. An agent hired for one transaction is a special agent.

45. D. Both the seller and the broker have an obligation to disclose material facts regarding the property's condition if they are known.

46. C. The definition of *market value* is specific as to it being the most probable price of a property. Sales price and market value are, one hopes, the same, but they don't have to be.

47. D. These are the four tests to determine the highest and best use for a piece of property.

48. B. The cost approach is used for new and unique properties. The gross rent multiplier and income capitalization approaches are used for income producing properties.

49. C. A condition of sale adjustment is made when a property has been sold under conditions other than an arm's-length transaction, such as a foreclosure, a condemnation, or a sale between relatives.

50. D. The other value principles may be at work in the value of the smaller home, but the specific positive effect referenced in the question is known as progression.

51. A. The principle of contribution is that an improvement to a property is worth what it adds to the overall value of the property, which may be higher, lower, or the same as its cost.

52. B. Choices A and C are types of depreciation and Choice D is a method to calculate deprecation. The usual term for the total of all types of depreciation is accrued.

53. D. The cutoff point for residential properties in federally related transactions is $250,000.

54. D. All of the conditions mentioned would render the sale suspect with respect to the price representing market value.

55. D. Replacement cost is for a duplicate building using updated materials. Rebuilding cost is not a term used in the cost approach. The depreciated cost comes after depreciation is deducted from either the reproduction or replacement cost.

56. B. The sales comparison method calls for differences between the comparable properties and the subject property to be accounted for by making adjustments to each comparable property individually to render it as much like the subject property as possible.

57. A. First you must multiply the $750 rental by 4 to account for the four units in the building: $750 × 4 = $3,000 gross monthly rent. The formula you want to use is Monthly Rental Income × Gross Rent Multiplier = Value, so $3,000 × 157 = $471,000.

58. D. The principle of substitution says that the maximum value of a property will be related to the cost of obtaining a property of similar usefulness.

59. B. Total depreciation from all sources, also known as accrued depreciation, is calculated on any building where it is present regardless of age and is then deducted from either the reproduction or replacement cost.

60. C. The value of the bedroom is added to the sales price of the comparable in order to make the comparable (three bedrooms) like the subject (four bedrooms): $225,000 + $30,000 = $255,000.

61. D. Generally, property values are best maintained and supported when they follow the principle of conformity in characteristics like size, design, and type of construction.

62. D. Curable and incurable with respect to an item of depreciation has nothing to do with whether the item can actually be repaired. The idea is based on whether the expenditure to repair something would add an equivalent value to the property (curable) or not (incurable). Therefore, cost and value in isolation from each other are incorrect answers.

63. B. Straight-line depreciation assumes that the entire cost of the house depreciates at an equal rate per year over the assumed lifetime (economic life) of the house. Reproduction or Replacement Cost of House ÷ Economic Life of House = Annual Depreciation, so $300,000 ÷ 50 years = $6,000 per year depreciation.

64. A. The shared appreciation mortgage requires some of the profit made when selling the house to be shared with the lender.

65. B. The role of the secondary market is to keep mortgage money in circulation by buying mortgage loans from primary lenders.

66. C. *Nonamortization* means none of the principal has been paid off during the life of the loan.

67. D. The way this question is worded, you could argue that all the answers are correct, but question writers will often ask questions like this meaning the lowest amount above which private mortgage insurance must be purchased.

68. A. A conforming loan meets FNMA underwriting standards and limits on the loan amount.

69. B. Real estate investments in general are not considered liquid (that is, quickly sold).

70. C. A foreclosure and a trustee's sale refer to basically the same action of selling the property when nonpayment of the mortgage loan occurs.

71. D. This is definitional.

72. D. California law (part of the real estate license law) sets limits of loan brokerage commissions.

73. C. FHA purchasers must invest a minimum of 3% of the purchase price.

74. B. A point is 1% of the loan amount.

$375,000 (Purchase Price) × 0.80 (Loan-to-Value Ratio) = $300,000 (Amount of Mortgage)

$300,000 (Amount of Mortgage) × 0.02 (Number of Points) = $6,000 (Amount Paid in Points)

Remember that to multiply percentages you have to convert to a decimal, so 80% = 0.80 and 2% = 0.02.

75. A. A holder in due course is someone who takes or purchases an existing note.

76. A. This is a primary difference between a mortgage and a trust deed.

77. A. All these terms relate in some way to foreclosure of trust deed sales but Choice A is the correct answer.

78. B. The Unruh Act extends this protection to homeowners.

79. C. The beneficiary is the lender.

80. D. Mortgage brokers arrange loans between lenders and borrowers.

81. C. The 30-year term is irrelevant.

$250,000 × 0.07 = $17,500 (First Year's Interest)

$17,500 ÷ 12 months = $1,458 (rounded)

82. B. The credit protection offered by the right to rescind does not extend to new purchases of property.

83. A. The Real Estate Settlement and Procedures Act requires the type of information described.

84. B. It must be completely handwritten by the maker of the will.

85. B. The soil deposited by the natural action of water is called alluvium or alluvion. These alluvial deposits are the by-products of the natural action of accretion. The loss of these alluvial deposits is known as *erosion* or in the case of a violent tearing away of the soil, *avulsion*. *Reliction* refers to the gradual lowering of the water level from the usual watermark. This would result in additional land being uncovered and are often referred to alluvion. Accretion is the legal concept whereby title to these alluvial deposits is transferred from one property owner to another.

86. A. This is definitional.

87. A. The person receiving the property need not sign the deed.

88. B. The quitclaim deed conveys whatever interest the owner has in the property without warranty.

89. C. Instructions given by the two parties jointly are called bilateral.

90. C. Referral or other fees may not be paid to anyone except the escrow agent's employees.

91. D. When documents have been recorded to the escrow agent's satisfaction, the escrow is closed.

92. C. The seller has paid the taxes for the current tax period. However, he will not own the house for the entire tax period. The buyer will owe the seller for a portion of the taxes already paid. The seller gets a credit and the buyer is charged with a debit. Remember that, unless otherwise stated in the problem, you have to assume that the buyer will pay for the day of closing.

$3,600 ÷ 12 months = $300 per month

$300 per month ÷ 30 days = $10 per day

The seller owns the property for 4 months and 14 days (since the closing is on the 15th). The buyer will own the property for 7 months and 16 days.

$300 per month × 7 months = $2,100

$10 per day × 16 = $160

$2,100 + $160 = $2,260 owed to the seller

93. B. The three correct terms refer to information kept on file at the title company's office for research purposes.

94. D. There is no standard as to who pays the premium throughout the state.

95. A. This factor has been established by law.

96. D. This is statutory.

97. D. The check can be held longer than the statutory three-day time period after acceptance of the offer if the principal authorizes it.

98. A. In order for an offer to be considered serious, it should have a deposit. The broker could do any of the other things to protect himself.

99. C. The 1866 Civil Rights Act prevents housing discrimination on the basis of race with no exceptions.

100. A. This is historical information.

101. C. This is the definition of blind advertising and is illegal.

102. A. The law requires at least one year.

103. D. The law requires that records be kept for three years if the transaction didn't close.

104. B. Although the relationship may differ for tax purposes, the state license law considers all salespeople employees for purposes of supervision.

105. D. Because a salesperson usually is an independent contractor, he can directly hire and compensate an unlicensed assistant.

106. D. This is the number required by law.

107. D. The commercial property restriction could, in fact, be a limitation to any particular kind of real estate activity.

108. D. This is statutory.

109. A. Technically, the applicant need not have *completed* the Real Estate Principles course to take the examination, but the applicant must at least be enrolled in it.

110. C. Being at least 18 is one of the requirements to obtain a real estate license. The phrasing "being only 18" was designed to lead you to think that 18 years old was to young. Watch out for tricky wording in questions.

111. C. A portion of real estate license fees go toward the fund.

112. B. There is no state code of ethics, but the state strongly suggests observance of the National Association of Realtors code of ethics.

113. B. Offers must continue to be presented. Although commissions are traditionally collected at closing. NAR does not mandate this. A Realtor should recommend the seller consult an attorney before accepting a subsequent offer.

114. A. This question is tricky, because all of the wrong answers are courses among the list of courses that can be selected to complete the requirements for a full license, but the license exam may be taken with just the Real Estate Principles course either completed or under way.

115. D. This is statutory.

116. D. This is statutory.

117. D. All the other choices are common practice and legal.

118. D. Choice B might be the confusing one, but because the lease will expire more than a year after it's signed, it must be in writing.

119. C. A material defect is usually related to the physical condition of the property itself. A material fact may be some other issue that affects the desirability of the property.

120. B. This is statutory.

121. D. This is statutory.

Practice Test 2

122. A. When a property is in escrow, it is still legally titled to the current property owner (the seller). The buyer has no title in the property whatsoever. However, the buyer does have an equitable interest in the property. Therefore, the seller would still have responsibility for any property damage that occurs before the close of escrow.

123. D. This is statutory.

124. A. This is statutory.

125. C. Because these are not violations of the details of the real estate law but rather violations of the overall law requiring a real estate license to perform certain activities, they are prosecuted locally by the district attorney.

126. D. This is definitional.

127. D. This is both statutory and a violation of recommended ethical practice.

128. D. This is statutory.

129. C. This is statutory. Choice D might seem logical but would likely only be an issue if additional funds were being sought from the owners to make needed repairs.

130. A. This is statutory.

131. A. This is statutory.

132. D. These disclosures are statutory under the right conditions. There is no such thing as demographic change disclosure.

133. B. Because all real estate sales contracts must be in writing, the contract is both void and unenforceable.

134. C. Don't be confused by Choice B. In both types of contracts, both parties agree to do something. The difference is stated in Choice C.

135. C. The suit for specific performance is the method for forcing a party to a contract to fulfill the terms of the contract.

136. B. Because the homeowner has expressed her terms and will pay only if a broker produces a buyer, Choice B is correct. The other answers are essentially random combinations of the terms involved in contracts and listings.

137. A. Although all the choices may be correct under certain circumstances, the most correct and that which is usually stated in the buyer-broker agreement is Choice A.

138. A. The acknowledgment is needed to file a deed.

139. C. The contract is valid because an emancipated minor is considered an adult and can enter into contracts.

140. A. The contract should say something about this situation to avoid a dispute.

141. B. This is statutory.

142. A. In the absence of a listing agreement, the broker must follow the buyer's instructions concerning depositing the buyer's funds into his trust account.

143. A. For leases less than a year, the law specifies payment of rent at the end of the term unless otherwise specified in the lease.

144. A. Novation is the signing of a new agreement to replace an old one.

145. A. This is statutory.

146. C. The other answers do not apply.

147. C. An option is the right to purchase the house not the obligation, so Choice D is wrong. Choice A is commonly called a rental option.

148. A. This is statutory.

149. D. The other types of loans could also have adjustable rate structures, but the adjustable or variable rate note protects the bank in the event that interest rates change over the life of the loan.

150. C. This is definitional.

Answer Sheet for Practice Test 3

(Remove This Sheet and Use It to Mark Your Answers)

1 Ⓐ Ⓑ Ⓒ Ⓓ	21 Ⓐ Ⓑ Ⓒ Ⓓ	41 Ⓐ Ⓑ Ⓒ Ⓓ	61 Ⓐ Ⓑ Ⓒ Ⓓ
2 Ⓐ Ⓑ Ⓒ Ⓓ	22 Ⓐ Ⓑ Ⓒ Ⓓ	42 Ⓐ Ⓑ Ⓒ Ⓓ	62 Ⓐ Ⓑ Ⓒ Ⓓ
3 Ⓐ Ⓑ Ⓒ Ⓓ	23 Ⓐ Ⓑ Ⓒ Ⓓ	43 Ⓐ Ⓑ Ⓒ Ⓓ	63 Ⓐ Ⓑ Ⓒ Ⓓ
4 Ⓐ Ⓑ Ⓒ Ⓓ	24 Ⓐ Ⓑ Ⓒ Ⓓ	44 Ⓐ Ⓑ Ⓒ Ⓓ	64 Ⓐ Ⓑ Ⓒ Ⓓ
5 Ⓐ Ⓑ Ⓒ Ⓓ	25 Ⓐ Ⓑ Ⓒ Ⓓ	45 Ⓐ Ⓑ Ⓒ Ⓓ	65 Ⓐ Ⓑ Ⓒ Ⓓ
6 Ⓐ Ⓑ Ⓒ Ⓓ	26 Ⓐ Ⓑ Ⓒ Ⓓ	46 Ⓐ Ⓑ Ⓒ Ⓓ	66 Ⓐ Ⓑ Ⓒ Ⓓ
7 Ⓐ Ⓑ Ⓒ Ⓓ	27 Ⓐ Ⓑ Ⓒ Ⓓ	47 Ⓐ Ⓑ Ⓒ Ⓓ	67 Ⓐ Ⓑ Ⓒ Ⓓ
8 Ⓐ Ⓑ Ⓒ Ⓓ	28 Ⓐ Ⓑ Ⓒ Ⓓ	48 Ⓐ Ⓑ Ⓒ Ⓓ	68 Ⓐ Ⓑ Ⓒ Ⓓ
9 Ⓐ Ⓑ Ⓒ Ⓓ	29 Ⓐ Ⓑ Ⓒ Ⓓ	49 Ⓐ Ⓑ Ⓒ Ⓓ	69 Ⓐ Ⓑ Ⓒ Ⓓ
10 Ⓐ Ⓑ Ⓒ Ⓓ	30 Ⓐ Ⓑ Ⓒ Ⓓ	50 Ⓐ Ⓑ Ⓒ Ⓓ	70 Ⓐ Ⓑ Ⓒ Ⓓ
11 Ⓐ Ⓑ Ⓒ Ⓓ	31 Ⓐ Ⓑ Ⓒ Ⓓ	51 Ⓐ Ⓑ Ⓒ Ⓓ	71 Ⓐ Ⓑ Ⓒ Ⓓ
12 Ⓐ Ⓑ Ⓒ Ⓓ	32 Ⓐ Ⓑ Ⓒ Ⓓ	52 Ⓐ Ⓑ Ⓒ Ⓓ	72 Ⓐ Ⓑ Ⓒ Ⓓ
13 Ⓐ Ⓑ Ⓒ Ⓓ	33 Ⓐ Ⓑ Ⓒ Ⓓ	53 Ⓐ Ⓑ Ⓒ Ⓓ	73 Ⓐ Ⓑ Ⓒ Ⓓ
14 Ⓐ Ⓑ Ⓒ Ⓓ	34 Ⓐ Ⓑ Ⓒ Ⓓ	54 Ⓐ Ⓑ Ⓒ Ⓓ	74 Ⓐ Ⓑ Ⓒ Ⓓ
15 Ⓐ Ⓑ Ⓒ Ⓓ	35 Ⓐ Ⓑ Ⓒ Ⓓ	55 Ⓐ Ⓑ Ⓒ Ⓓ	75 Ⓐ Ⓑ Ⓒ Ⓓ
16 Ⓐ Ⓑ Ⓒ Ⓓ	36 Ⓐ Ⓑ Ⓒ Ⓓ	56 Ⓐ Ⓑ Ⓒ Ⓓ	76 Ⓐ Ⓑ Ⓒ Ⓓ
17 Ⓐ Ⓑ Ⓒ Ⓓ	37 Ⓐ Ⓑ Ⓒ Ⓓ	57 Ⓐ Ⓑ Ⓒ Ⓓ	77 Ⓐ Ⓑ Ⓒ Ⓓ
18 Ⓐ Ⓑ Ⓒ Ⓓ	38 Ⓐ Ⓑ Ⓒ Ⓓ	58 Ⓐ Ⓑ Ⓒ Ⓓ	78 Ⓐ Ⓑ Ⓒ Ⓓ
19 Ⓐ Ⓑ Ⓒ Ⓓ	39 Ⓐ Ⓑ Ⓒ Ⓓ	59 Ⓐ Ⓑ Ⓒ Ⓓ	79 Ⓐ Ⓑ Ⓒ Ⓓ
20 Ⓐ Ⓑ Ⓒ Ⓓ	40 Ⓐ Ⓑ Ⓒ Ⓓ	60 Ⓐ Ⓑ Ⓒ Ⓓ	80 Ⓐ Ⓑ Ⓒ Ⓓ

81 Ⓐ Ⓑ Ⓒ Ⓓ	101 Ⓐ Ⓑ Ⓒ Ⓓ	121 Ⓐ Ⓑ Ⓒ Ⓓ	141 Ⓐ Ⓑ Ⓒ Ⓓ
82 Ⓐ Ⓑ Ⓒ Ⓓ	102 Ⓐ Ⓑ Ⓒ Ⓓ	122 Ⓐ Ⓑ Ⓒ Ⓓ	142 Ⓐ Ⓑ Ⓒ Ⓓ
83 Ⓐ Ⓑ Ⓒ Ⓓ	103 Ⓐ Ⓑ Ⓒ Ⓓ	123 Ⓐ Ⓑ Ⓒ Ⓓ	143 Ⓐ Ⓑ Ⓒ Ⓓ
84 Ⓐ Ⓑ Ⓒ Ⓓ	104 Ⓐ Ⓑ Ⓒ Ⓓ	124 Ⓐ Ⓑ Ⓒ Ⓓ	144 Ⓐ Ⓑ Ⓒ Ⓓ
85 Ⓐ Ⓑ Ⓒ Ⓓ	105 Ⓐ Ⓑ Ⓒ Ⓓ	125 Ⓐ Ⓑ Ⓒ Ⓓ	145 Ⓐ Ⓑ Ⓒ Ⓓ
86 Ⓐ Ⓑ Ⓒ Ⓓ	106 Ⓐ Ⓑ Ⓒ Ⓓ	126 Ⓐ Ⓑ Ⓒ Ⓓ	146 Ⓐ Ⓑ Ⓒ Ⓓ
87 Ⓐ Ⓑ Ⓒ Ⓓ	107 Ⓐ Ⓑ Ⓒ Ⓓ	127 Ⓐ Ⓑ Ⓒ Ⓓ	147 Ⓐ Ⓑ Ⓒ Ⓓ
88 Ⓐ Ⓑ Ⓒ Ⓓ	108 Ⓐ Ⓑ Ⓒ Ⓓ	128 Ⓐ Ⓑ Ⓒ Ⓓ	148 Ⓐ Ⓑ Ⓒ Ⓓ
89 Ⓐ Ⓑ Ⓒ Ⓓ	109 Ⓐ Ⓑ Ⓒ Ⓓ	129 Ⓐ Ⓑ Ⓒ Ⓓ	149 Ⓐ Ⓑ Ⓒ Ⓓ
90 Ⓐ Ⓑ Ⓒ Ⓓ	110 Ⓐ Ⓑ Ⓒ Ⓓ	130 Ⓐ Ⓑ Ⓒ Ⓓ	150 Ⓐ Ⓑ Ⓒ Ⓓ
91 Ⓐ Ⓑ Ⓒ Ⓓ	111 Ⓐ Ⓑ Ⓒ Ⓓ	131 Ⓐ Ⓑ Ⓒ Ⓓ	
92 Ⓐ Ⓑ Ⓒ Ⓓ	112 Ⓐ Ⓑ Ⓒ Ⓓ	132 Ⓐ Ⓑ Ⓒ Ⓓ	
93 Ⓐ Ⓑ Ⓒ Ⓓ	113 Ⓐ Ⓑ Ⓒ Ⓓ	133 Ⓐ Ⓑ Ⓒ Ⓓ	
94 Ⓐ Ⓑ Ⓒ Ⓓ	114 Ⓐ Ⓑ Ⓒ Ⓓ	134 Ⓐ Ⓑ Ⓒ Ⓓ	
95 Ⓐ Ⓑ Ⓒ Ⓓ	115 Ⓐ Ⓑ Ⓒ Ⓓ	135 Ⓐ Ⓑ Ⓒ Ⓓ	
96 Ⓐ Ⓑ Ⓒ Ⓓ	116 Ⓐ Ⓑ Ⓒ Ⓓ	136 Ⓐ Ⓑ Ⓒ Ⓓ	
97 Ⓐ Ⓑ Ⓒ Ⓓ	117 Ⓐ Ⓑ Ⓒ Ⓓ	137 Ⓐ Ⓑ Ⓒ Ⓓ	
98 Ⓐ Ⓑ Ⓒ Ⓓ	118 Ⓐ Ⓑ Ⓒ Ⓓ	138 Ⓐ Ⓑ Ⓒ Ⓓ	
99 Ⓐ Ⓑ Ⓒ Ⓓ	119 Ⓐ Ⓑ Ⓒ Ⓓ	139 Ⓐ Ⓑ Ⓒ Ⓓ	
100 Ⓐ Ⓑ Ⓒ Ⓓ	120 Ⓐ Ⓑ Ⓒ Ⓓ	140 Ⓐ Ⓑ Ⓒ Ⓓ	

CUT HERE

Practice Test 3

Directions: For each of the following questions, select the choice that best answers the question.

1. Which of the following is not true about the rights of a tenant in a lease situation?

   A. The tenant has a less than freehold estate.
   B. The tenant has a leasehold interest.
   C. The interest that the tenant has is considered personal property.
   D. The tenant has a fee simple defeasible interest.

2. A landowner's subsurface rights include everything except

   A. rights to the center of the Earth.
   B. rights to drill vertically for oil and gas.
   C. rights to drill at a slant onto a neighbor's property for oil and gas.
   D. all minerals that can be extracted from underground.

3. The stock in a mutual water company that is appurtenant to the land

   A. may be transferred with no restrictions.
   B. may only be transferred back to the mutual water company.
   C. may only be transferred with the transfer of the property.
   D. may not be transferred.

4. In a real estate sale, fixtures

   A. are assumed to stay with the property.
   B. are assumed to go with the seller.
   C. are considered personal property.
   D. must be transferred with a separate bill of sale.

5. In the government or rectangular survey system, which of the following is not true?

   A. A section is 640 acres.
   B. A township has 36 sections.
   C. A section is a square ½-mile on each side.
   D. A township is a square 6 miles on each side.

6. In the government survey system, when, because of natural features, a lot less than a quarter section was created, it was referred to as a(n)

   A. odd lot.
   B. survey lot.
   C. substandard lot.
   D. government lot.

GO ON TO THE NEXT PAGE

7. An assessor's map may not be used to legally describe a property in a deed unless the map

    A. has been filed in the county recorder's office.

    B. has been filed in the assessor's office.

    C. shows new boundary information not previously recorded.

    D. None of the above—it can always be used to legally describe property.

8. Concurrent ownership means

    A. property owned by more than one person at the same time.

    B. property owned by one person.

    C. property owned by individuals one after the other.

    D. property only owned by a married couple.

9. Upon the death of a person who owns property in joint tenancy, her interest goes to

    A. her devisees.

    B. the surviving joint tenants.

    C. her heirs.

    D. any tenants in common.

10. A husband owns a rental building that he acquired before he got married. During the course of the marriage, he sells the building and buys another building. The new building he has acquired is considered

    A. separate property.

    B. community property.

    C. partial community property.

    D. joint property.

11. Which of the following is not true when holding title to real property in co-ownership as tenancy in partnership?

    A. The partners' interest in rents or profits must be equal.

    B. The entire property is vulnerable for the debts of the partnership.

    C. Upon the death of a partner, his interest goes to the surviving partner(s).

    D. A partner's right in the real property would be subject to community property rules.

12. Which of the following is true regarding an encumbrance?

    A. All encumbrances are financial claims against the property.

    B. All encumbrances are physical limitations on the property.

    C. All encumbrances will stop a transfer of title to the property.

    D. All encumbrances are the interest of someone other than the title holder.

13. Design professionals such as architects

    A. are specifically prohibited from seeking a mechanic's lien.

    B. are specifically permitted to seek a mechanic's lien.

    C. may seek a mechanic's lien only on a construction project that has been completed.

    D. are permitted to seek a mechanic's lien without prior notice of default.

14. Landowner A gives Landowner B a permanent right to cross her property with a driveway so Landowner B can get to the highway. Which of the following describes this relationship?

    A. Landowner A is the dominant tenement and Landowner B is the servient tenement.

    B. This relationship is a license and, therefore, carries no interest in the real estate.

    C. This relationship is an easement in gross.

    D. Landowner B is the dominant tenement and Landowner A is the servient tenement.

15. A deed restriction requiring that a house be of a minimum size will be

    A. valid.

    B. void.

    C. unenforceable.

    D. a violation of fair housing laws.

16. Deed restrictions are also known as

    A. enhanced zoning.

    B. special permit provisions.

    C. variances.

    D. private contract restrictions.

17. A limited partner's liability in a real estate investment is

    A. the same as a general partner's.

    B. limited to the amount of his investment.

    C. limited as long as he assumes some responsibilities for management.

    D. limited to the limited partner's proportionate share of the overall partnership's liability.

18. A government document addressing the future physical development, transportation, housing, and other issues is called the

    A. zoning ordinance.

    B. general plan.

    C. building code.

    D. subdivision map law.

Practice Test 3

GO ON TO THE NEXT PAGE

19. The authority to adopt zoning ordinances is derived from the

 A. police power.
 B. eminent domain law.
 C. law of escheat.
 D. subdivision laws.

20. Funeral homes are listed in the zoning ordinance as a permitted use in some residential areas provided certain specific requirements are met. Someone wanting to build a funeral home in such a residential area will most likely have to apply for a(n)

 A. exception permit.
 B. use variance.
 C. area variance.
 D. conditional use permit.

21. Which of the following types of projects would least likely be subject to CEQA requirements?

 A. building permit for a single-family house
 B. development plan for a large shopping center
 C. adoption of a new zoning ordinance
 D. approval of a tentative subdivision plan

22. A person attempting to use property in a way that is not consistent with the principal uses listed in the zoning ordinance might use any of the following except a

 A. conditional use permit.
 B. zoning variance.
 C. rezoning of the area.
 D. planned unit development.

23. In a trust ownership situation, title is held by the trustee on behalf of the

 A. trustor.
 B. grantee.
 C. beneficiary.
 D. grantor.

24. Which of the following is not actually a legal form of property ownership or real estate investment?

 A. limited liability company
 B. limited partnership
 C. S corporation
 D. syndicate

25. The action required to dissolve a tenants-in-common ownership if the owners cannot reach an agreement is called

   A. separation.

   B. partition.

   C. participation.

   D. possession.

26. Two types of property interest provide for possession but not ownership. They are

   A. fee simple absolute and leasehold.

   B. fee simple and life estate.

   C. freehold and leasehold.

   D. leasehold and life estate.

27. The N ½ of the W ½ of the SE ¼ of a section of land contains how many acres?

   A. 640 acres

   B. 320 acres

   C. 160 acres

   D. 40 acres

28. Compensation from the Real Estate Recovery Account is limited to how much per transaction?

   A. $5,000

   B. $10,000

   C. $15,000

   D. $20,000

29. Broker A is hired by Seller B to market her property for $300,000. Broker A decides to buy the property himself and pays full price. A week later, Broker A sells the property for $325,000. Which of the following statements is true?

   A. Broker A did nothing wrong, since he paid the seller what she wanted.

   B. Broker should have shared the $25,000 profit with the seller.

   C. Broker A should have told the seller of the deal he was going to make and gotten her permission.

   D. It was a conflict of interest for Broker A to buy the property, and he should not have done it.

30. Real estate commissions are

   A. set by the California Real Estate Commission.

   B. set by the local multiple listing service.

   C. always based on a percentage of the property's sale price.

   D. negotiable.

Practice Test 3

GO ON TO THE NEXT PAGE

31. How long after the acceptance of an offer does a broker have in which to place a buyer's deposit check into an escrow account?

  A. one business day after the acceptance of an offer

  B. three business days after the acceptance of an offer

  C. five business days after the acceptance of an offer

  D. up to ten business days before title closes

32. The right of an agent to do something in the sale of a property that is not specified in the listing agreement but is accepted practice is known as

  A. apparent authority.

  B. inherent authority.

  C. actual authority.

  D. functional authority.

33. Commingling is

  A. mixing client funds with the broker's own funds.

  B. illegal.

  C. avoided by depositing the funds in an escrow account.

  D. all of the above

34. The only type of agency agreement that need not be in writing or confirmed in writing is

  A. agency by estoppel.

  B. agency by ratification.

  C. implied agency.

  D. None of the above—all agency agreements must be in writing.

35. An open listing is an

  A. express unilateral contract.

  B. express bilateral contract.

  C. implied unilateral contract.

  D. implied bilateral contract.

36. ABC Real Estate Company withholds Social Security from its workers' pay, pays unemployment insurance on their behalf, and withholds payroll taxes. The workers are most likely

  A. employees.

  B. independent contractors.

  C. employees for real estate purposes but independent contractors for tax purposes.

  D. free to decide their category of employment based on which benefits them the most.

37. Cooperating brokers represent

- **A.** the buyer.
- **B.** the seller.
- **C.** both the buyer and the seller.
- **D.** whomever they have an agency agreement with.

38. Pocket listings are

- **A.** illegal.
- **B.** unethical.
- **C.** not a problem.
- **D.** governed by multiple listing service rules.

39. The difference between an employee and an independent contractor for tax purposes is

- **A.** the number of hours worked per week.
- **B.** the amount of direct supervision provided by the broker.
- **C.** the taxes withheld by the broker.
- **D.** whether the agent is paid a flat fee per sale or a percentage commission.

40. Buyers' brokers may be paid by

- **A.** only buyers.
- **B.** only sellers.
- **C.** either buyers or sellers.
- **D.** cooperating brokers.

41. Broker A takes a listing to sell a house. Broker B brings a buyer to see the house and prepares an offer on behalf of the buyer. What do we know for certain about Broker B?

- **A.** She is a subagent of Broker A.
- **B.** She is a buyer's broker representing the buyer.
- **C.** She is a cooperating broker.
- **D.** She is a dual agent representing both seller and buyer.

42. The fact that a salesperson must always work under a broker's supervision makes it mandatory that, for certain purposes, the salesperson is considered

- **A.** an employee.
- **B.** an independent contractor.
- **C.** either an employee or an independent contractor.
- **D.** an agent.

GO ON TO THE NEXT PAGE

Practice Test 3

43. A written disclosure of agency relationships must be presented to the seller before

- **A.** the seller signs the listing agreement.
- **B.** the seller accepts an offer to purchase.
- **C.** the seller signs a contract of sale.
- **D.** the closing.

44. A broker who is acting both as principal and agent

- **A.** is a dual agent.
- **B.** may be exercising an option listing agreement.
- **C.** has some form of exclusive listing agreement.
- **D.** is always breaking the law.

45. For which of the following activities would the broker not require specific authority from the principal?

- **A.** to use the services of an administrative assistant to prepare the sales brochure for the house
- **B.** to work with cooperating brokers
- **C.** to place the listing into the multiple listing service system
- **D.** to place a FOR SALE sign on the lawn

46. Which of the following best describes the type of income used in the income capitalization approach?

- **A.** potential gross income
- **B.** potential rental income
- **C.** scheduled gross income
- **D.** scheduled rental income

47. An appraiser asked to appraise a church would most likely use what valuation approach?

- **A.** income capitalization approach
- **B.** cost approach
- **C.** gross rent multiplier approach
- **D.** sales comparison approach

48. The value of the largest house located in a neighborhood of smaller homes may be affected according to the principle of

- **A.** conformity.
- **B.** anticipation.
- **C.** regression.
- **D.** supply and demand.

49. In the sales comparison approach, the value of a feature present in a comparable that is not present in the subject is

    A. added to the selling price of the subject.

    B. subtracted from the selling price of the subject.

    C. added to the selling price of the comparable.

    D. subtracted from the selling price of the comparable.

50. Which of the following is not a characteristic of value?

    A. demand

    B. transferability

    C. utility

    D. anticipation

51. Spending money to improve a property beyond the point where the improvements add value to the property is an example of the principle of

    A. change.

    B. progression.

    C. diminishing returns.

    D. supply and demand.

52. A relatively new house contains 2,500 square feet of space. A similar, 2,600-square-foot house built recently cost $338,000 to build, excluding the land costs. What is the estimated reproduction cost of the 2,500-square-foot house?

    A. $338,000

    B. $325,000

    C. $310,000

    D. $300,000

53. Functional utility can best be described as

    A. overall usefulness of the property.

    B. condition of the property.

    C. design features that meet market demand.

    D. curb appeal.

54. Net operating income does not include consideration of which of the following?

    A. vacancy rates

    B. mortgage payments

    C. operating expenses

    D. property taxes

Practice Test 3

GO ON TO THE NEXT PAGE

55. The method for estimating reproduction or replacement cost that is most useful as a check on the other appraisal methods is the

A. historic cost index method.
B. quantity survey method.
C. unit in place method.
D. square foot method.

56. The estimated cost to build a 200-year-old house using modern materials and construction methods is called its

A. replacement cost.
B. reproduction cost.
C. rebuilding cost.
D. current cost.

57. When the supply of houses goes up and the demand stays the same, what will likely happen to house prices?

A. Prices go up.
B. Prices go down.
C. Prices stay the same.
D. none of the above

58. The estimated reproduction cost of a house is $200,000. The estimated depreciation on the house is 30%. What is the depreciated cost of the house?

A. $60,000
B. $140,000
C. $200,000
D. $260,000

59. A comparable property sold six months ago for $250,000. Prices of similar properties have increased by 5% since that time. At what amount would a broker doing a competitive market analysis on a similar house likely value the subject property?

A. $237,500
B. $250,000
C. $262,500
D. $312,500

60. The average sales price for your subject property is $300,000, which is 10% below the asking price after three months on the market. The house you are looking at to use as a comparable for your competitive market analysis sold at full asking price, after only two weeks on the market. Is this property a good comparable sale for you to use in your CMA?

A. Yes, because whatever price a house sells for is its market value.
B. Yes, because you can adjust for whatever factors are different.
C. No, because it likely sold below market value.
D. No, because it sold at asking price.

61. An oversupply of condominiums built in a retirement area is often the result of not paying attention to the principle of

    A. competition.

    B. regression.

    C. highest and best use.

    D. contribution.

62. Value can best be described as

    A. value in use.

    B. assessed value.

    C. market value.

    D. value in exchange.

63. The effects of natural phenomena like earthquakes and market forces can best be described as the effects of the principle of

    A. supply and demand.

    B. change.

    C. competition.

    D. anticipation.

64. An acceleration clause in a mortgage loan or trust deed

    A. allows the borrower to make advance payments on principal.

    B. allows the borrower to renegotiate the interest rate.

    C. allows the lender to sell the loan to another lender.

    D. allows the lender to declare the entire loan amount due immediately.

65. A real estate broker discusses a buyer's mortgage needs with her, advising her of the types of loans available for her particular circumstances and suggesting a lender who might accommodate her needs. The agent even enters the buyer's information into a computerized system to help the lender provide the type of financing needed. Which of the following is true regarding payment of a fee by the lender to the real estate broker?

    A. This fee would be a kickback and is illegal.

    B. The fee could be paid.

    C. The fee could be paid, but only if the broker were also an employee of the lender.

    D. The fee could only be paid if the loan actually went through.

GO ON TO THE NEXT PAGE

66. Among other activities, which of the following does the Federal Reserve System do to control the supply of money available for loans?

    A. print money

    B. control the rate at which the secondary market may purchase loans

    C. set the discount rate

    D. set the inflation rate

67. Which of the following will be affected by California usury laws?

    A. a loan arranged by a real estate broker to buy property

    B. a seller taking back a mortgage as part of the purchase price on a house

    C. a bank making a real estate loan

    D. a private lender making a loan to buy a house

68. In a loan situation, what does a mortgage do?

    A. It provides the lender with a promise to pay.

    B. It sets the terms of the loan.

    C. It turns over title to the property until the loan is paid off.

    D. It acts as the security instrument for the loan.

69. When two people cosign a note that requires joint and several liability, it means that

    A. each cosigner is responsible for half the loan amount regardless of his shares in the property.

    B. each cosigner may be responsible for the entire loan but only if the other cosigner dies.

    C. each cosigner can be required to pay the entire loan amount if the other defaults.

    D. each cosigner is responsible for the whole debt but only if the cosigners hold the title in joint ownership.

70. Due to an increase in his home's value, a homeowner refinances his home for an amount larger than the original mortgage. After a few years, his financial situation changes and he can no longer make his mortgage payments. Due to a downturn in the marketplace, the foreclosure sale of the house does not cover the amount of the mortgage. His lender can

    A. do nothing because of the antideficiency law.

    B. sue for a deficiency judgment.

    C. do nothing unless the lender applied for a judicial foreclosure.

    D. do nothing unless it was a mortgage loan rather than a trust deed situation.

71. Which of the following is correct?

   A. A mortgagee borrows money from a mortgagor.
   B. A trustee conveys title to a beneficiary upon payment of the debt by the trustor.
   C. A trustor conveys title to a trustee on behalf of a beneficiary.
   D. A trustee and a mortgagee are essentially the same.

72. A holder in due course would probably not be able to enforce a note if the note maker used a defense of

   A. prior payment.
   B. cancellation.
   C. lack of consideration.
   D. forgery.

73. A deed in lieu of foreclosure

   A. will avoid a foreclosure sale.
   B. is executed after the foreclosure sale.
   C. benefits the beneficiary if the property is worth less than the amount owed on the mortgage.
   D. is the same as a reconveyance deed.

74. A buyer purchases a property for $260,000 with 100% financing and is required to obtain private mortgage insurance (PMI). Assuming the property's value has not changed, at what point will the buyer be able to stop paying for the PMI?

   A. when he has paid off $130,000
   B. when he has paid off $85,800
   C. when he has paid off $78,000
   D. when he has paid off $65,000

75. In the case of a VA loan where the buyer signed a contract prior to receiving a CRV, what are the buyer's rights?

   A. He can cancel the contract when he receives the CRV.
   B. He can cancel the contract within five days of receiving the CRV.
   C. He can cancel the contract if the CRV is less than the purchase price if such a contingency is written into the contract.
   D. None of the above—the buyer has no right to cancel under any circumstances.

76. Which of the following types of mortgage loans do not fall under RESPA requirements?

   A. VA loans
   B. FHA loans
   C. bank loans being sold to FNMA
   D. private loans being retained by the lender

GO ON TO THE NEXT PAGE

77. A person making loans on owner-occupied residential property fewer than how many times a year is exempt from Regulation Z?

A. 6
B. 10
C. 20
D. 25

78. Which of the following is true of VA loans?

A. The buyer cannot pay more than the appraised value.
B. The VA requires a down payment.
C. The VA guarantee can be for more than the appraised value.
D. The lender can require a down payment.

79. The VA permits refinancing under all except which of the following conditions?

A. to fund education
B. to secure a lower interest rate
C. to purchase a second investment property home
D. to finance an amount no greater than the original loan

80. The secondary mortgage market includes all of the following except

A. FNMA.
B. FDIC.
C. GNMA.
D. FHLMC.

81. What clause in the original mortgage loan or trust deed would prevent the use of a wraparound mortgage by a seller?

A. due-on-sale clause
B. acceleration clause
C. contingency clause
D. prepayment penalty clause

82. A deed of reconveyance is used to

A. convey title from the trustor to the trustee.
B. convey title from the beneficiary to the trustor.
C. convey title from the trustee to the trustor.
D. convey title from the beneficiary to the successful bidder in a foreclosure sale.

83. A security instrument in a loan

   A. hypothecates the property.
   B. subordinates the property.
   C. forecloses the property.
   D. redeems the property.

84. According to the laws of intestate succession, where there is community property owned by Spouse A and Spouse B, in the event of the death of Spouse A, Spouse A's half of the property will

   A. be divided among the children.
   B. go to Spouse B.
   C. go to whomever is named as heir in the will.
   D. be divided equally among the children and Spouse B.

85. Increasing the value of a property by constructing a building on it is called

   A. accretion.
   B. reliction.
   C. avulsion.
   D. improvement.

86. Owner A buys property near a lake and crosses his neighbor's property every day for more than five years to get to the lake. At this point, having never discussed the matter with his neighbor, Owner A has most likely acquired what with respect to his neighbor's property?

   A. ownership by adverse possession
   B. ownership by prescription
   C. easement by prescription
   D. easement by private grant

87. In researching a chain of title on a piece of property being sold, which of the following is true?

   A. The current grantor was the previous grantee.
   B. The current grantee was the previous grantee.
   C. The current grantee was the previous grantor.
   D. The current grantor was the previous grantor.

88. The warrantees in a grant deed are

   A. expressed.
   B. implied.
   C. guaranteed.
   D. insured.

GO ON TO THE NEXT PAGE

89. Escrow agents are licensed by the

    A. State Department of Banking.

    B. California Real Estate Commission.

    C. Department of Corporations.

    D. state attorney general.

90. If a property is purchased subject to an existing mortgage loan, the escrow agent will ask the lender for a(n)

    A. demand for payoff.

    B. beneficiary statement.

    C. trust deed.

    D. estoppel certificate.

91. The apportionment of tax payments at closing is known as

    A. division.

    B. allocation.

    C. apportionment.

    D. proration.

92. Fuel oil left in the tank at the time of closing is best described as a

    A. credit to the seller.

    B. debit to the seller.

    C. credit to the buyer.

    D. proration.

93. Paying referral fees for directing title insurance business is

    A. legal.

    B. illegal.

    C. legal, as long as the fee is paid to a license holder.

    D. legal, but only if paid to an escrow agent.

94. The premium for the title insurance insuring the lender is generally paid by the

    A. buyer.

    B. seller.

    C. lender.

    D. FHA.

95. For purposes of taxation, assuming a property transfer is not recorded, how many days after the transfer in ownership does the new owner have to file the change in property ownership statement with the recorder or the assessor?

A. 15
B. 30
C. 45
D. 60

96. When is a tax lien placed on a property?

A. January 1, when the assessment roll takes effect
B. November 1, when the first tax installment is due
C. February 1, when the second tax installment is due
D. January 1 of the following year if the previous year's taxes have not been paid

97. An offer to purchase that is not accepted by the seller would result in the deposit funds being

A. deposited in the trust account.
B. sent to the escrow agent.
C. returned to the buyer.
D. held by the broker.

98. Commingling of funds is permitted

A. when the offer is accepted.
B. before the offer is accepted.
C. within three days of the offer being accepted.
D. never.

99. An exemption to the federal Fair Housing Act of 1968 is provided to

A. no one.
B. religious organizations providing housing to its members.
C. subdivisions of fewer than ten houses.
D. owner-occupied apartment houses of fewer than eight units.

100. The practice of discrimination in lending policies based on location is known as

A. steering.
B. blockbusting.
C. redlining.
D. underwriting.

GO ON TO THE NEXT PAGE

101. A home having two scraggly bushes and a lightning-damaged tree is advertised by the broker as having beautiful landscaping. The broker is most likely guilty of

    A. misrepresentation and could lose his license.

    B. puffing and will not lose his license.

    C. exaggeration and will probably have to pay for additional landscaping.

    D. nothing.

102. A blind ad in a newspaper is acceptable

    A. if a sign is placed on the property identifying the broker.

    B. if the property is also listed in the multiple listing service system.

    C. if the property is listed on a Web site with the broker's name.

    D. under no circumstances.

103. Almost three years to the date after listing a property that a broker sold, the broker is asked to produce the records of the transaction. He is unable to because he cleaned out his files. Has the broker violated the law?

    A. No, because he kept the files for three years from the listing date.

    B. No, because he only needs to keep the files one year from the listing or closing date.

    C. No, because he only needs to keep the files three years from the listing or closing date.

    D. Yes, because he needs to keep the files three years from the closing date unless the property didn't close.

104. A written employment agreement between a salesperson and a broker is

    A. optional.

    B. mandatory.

    C. only required for employees.

    D. only required for independent contractors.

105. Which of the following tasks can an unlicensed assistant not perform?

    A. creating advertising brochures

    B. preparing rent receipts and escrow account information

    C. meeting the appraiser at the property

    D. driving buyers around to different houses

106. How many members of the California Real Estate Advisory Commission must be licensed brokers?

    A. four

    B. six

    C. seven

    D. ten

107. If a real estate license is revoked, how long must the licensee wait to reapply for a license?

   A. five years

   B. three years

   C. one year

   D. six months

108. Which of the following is not a license law violation?

   A. having no termination date on a listing agreement

   B. offering a rebate or gift to a prospective client

   C. misrepresenting a property defect

   D. failing to disclose a property defect

109. Which of the following persons would not be exempt from real estate licensing requirements?

   A. an attorney selling a house on behalf of an estate he is administering.

   B. a trustee selling a deed of trust

   C. a bank loan officer selling a foreclosed property

   D. a property manager managing ten buildings for five different clients.

110. Illegal immigrants may

   A. not obtain a real estate license.

   B. obtain a real estate license with no restrictions.

   C. obtain a conditional real estate license.

   D. obtain a temporary, 150-day real estate license.

111. Buyer A has received an award from the State Real Estate Recovery Account as a result of circumstances involving Broker B. As a result,

   A. Broker B's license is suspended.

   B. Broker B's license is revoked.

   C. Broker B will face criminal charges.

   D. Broker B has a 90-day grace period in which to reimburse the fund.

112. Under which of the following circumstances, according to the NAR code of ethics, may a Realtor reveal confidential information?

   A. when presented with a court order

   B. when the Realtor has been given the full informed consent of the client

   C. when the client intends to commit a crime

   D. all of the above

GO ON TO THE NEXT PAGE

Practice Test 3

113. A real estate broker must disclose all but which of the following to his seller client?

    A. that he intends to cooperate with other brokers in selling the property

    B. the specific nature of the advertising to be done

    C. that the seller may compensate the buyer's agent

    D. the potential, if any, that the broker may act as a dual agent

114. The major difference between a real estate broker and a real estate salesperson is that the

    A. broker can accept commissions from a client the salesperson cannot.

    B. broker can be an agent the salesperson cannot.

    C. broker can be a Realtor the salesperson cannot.

    D. salesperson is an independent contractor the broker is not.

115. The prepaid rental listing service license requires a surety bond of

    A. $10,000.

    B. $5,000.

    C. $3,000.

    D. $1,000.

116. A California real estate broker is negotiating with someone in San Francisco to buy property in Nevada. California requires him to have

    A. nothing more than his California broker's license.

    B. at least a Nevada real estate broker's license.

    C. both California and Nevada broker's licenses.

    D. a California broker's license and at least a Nevada salesperson's license.

117. An attorney in fact

    A. may be an attorney-at-law.

    B. should at least have gone to law school even if he hasn't passed the bar.

    C. may be authorized by a power of attorney to act on the behalf of a principal in certain matters.

    D. must be appointed by the court.

118. If a lease for an apartment does not specify the length of tenancy, it is presumed to be

    A. an estate for years.

    B. for a one-year term.

    C. month to month.

    D. one year and one day.

119. Which of the following is a disclosable material fact?

   A. A murder was committed on the property five years earlier.

   B. The previous owner died of AIDS.

   C. A new bedroom was added onto the house by the current owner.

   D. The town is planning to build a new park a mile away from the house.

120. The obligation of a real estate agent to inspect a property for material defects extends to

   A. one-family houses only.

   B. one- to four-family houses only.

   C. commercial properties only.

   D. all residential and commercial properties.

121. Who is responsible for disclosing material defects and material facts to the buyer?

   A. the seller

   B. the seller's agent

   C. the buyer's agent

   D. all of the above

122. A buyer moves into a seller's property two weeks before escrow closes. The buyer would most likely be a(n)

   A. tenant.

   B. equity holder.

   C. trustee.

   D. beneficiary.

123. The California Real Estate Recovery Account is designed to compensate victims of all but which of the following?

   A. fraud

   B. conversion of trust funds

   C. misrepresentation

   D. physical injury

124. When a payment is made on behalf of a licensee from the recovery account, what must occur before the licensee's license can be reinstated?

   A. One year must pass.

   B. The licensee must reimburse the trust fund the full amount paid.

   C. The licensee must reimburse the trust fund at least half of the amount paid.

   D. No reinstatement is necessary since the licensee's license is usually not suspended.

GO ON TO THE NEXT PAGE

Practice Test 3

125. Which of the following activities would not require a real estate license?

    A. selling homes for another person
    B. brokering mortgages
    C. selling your own commercial property
    D. managing several single-family home rentals for another person

126. A one-family home is sold "as is" by a homeowner. Which of the following disclosures will not be required?

    A. agency disclosure
    B. lead-paint disclosure
    C. property condition transfer disclosure statement
    D. natural hazard disclosure statement

127. How many members other than the commissioner are on the California Real Estate Advisory Commission?

    A. five
    B. seven
    C. nine
    D. ten

128. The lead-based paint disclosure law requires

    A. sellers to complete the disclosure form.
    B. brokers to complete the disclosure form.
    C. that buyers be given ten days to have the house tested.
    D. sellers to have the house tested for lead-based paint hazards.

129. Disclosures of seismic hazards and earthquake fault areas are

    A. mandatory.
    B. covered by the same legislation.
    C. only mandatory for structures over four stories high.
    D. only mandatory for buildings built before 1980.

130. The public report for a condominium will include

    A. interest to be acquired by the purchaser.
    B. negative environmental issues.
    C. limitations on the use of the property.
    D. all of the above

131. Although not mandatory, which of the following disclosures would most likely be made if the condition existed?

   A. natural hazard disclosure

   B. earthquake fault zone disclosure

   C. mold disclosure

   D. lead-based paint disclosure

132. Which of the following does not exist?

   A. Alquist-Priolo Earthquake Fault Zoning Act

   B. Seismic Hazards Mapping Act

   C. Environmental Assessment Reporting Act

   D. Coastal Zone Conservation Act

133. A contract made while one of the parties was drunk may still be valid if the contract

   A. was made in writing.

   B. was made in front of witnesses.

   C. is affirmed when the person is sober.

   D. was for something other than real estate.

134. Which of the following types of contracts need not be in writing?

   A. sales of real estate

   B. listings of real estate for sale

   C. leases for one year

   D. leases for more than one year

135. The best way to discharge a contract is

   A. performance.

   B. release.

   C. reformation.

   D. rescission.

136. A broker brings a buyer to a home that has been advertised as for sale by owner, discusses various sales-related matters with the owner, and offers the owner advice that the owner accepts. The sale goes through. Because nothing was ever put in writing between the broker and the owner, what type of agreement did the broker have with the owner?

   A. implied, unilateral, valid

   B. implied, bilateral, invalid

   C. expressed, bilateral, valid

   D. implied, unilateral, invalid

GO ON TO THE NEXT PAGE

Practice Test 3

137. A buyer's broker is representing two buyers for the same house. This is

    A. a possible dual agency.

    B. never acceptable.

    C. permitted if both agree.

    D. both A and C

138. Which of the following is correct with respect to making an offer to purchase real estate?

    A. An offeror makes the offer; an offeree receives the offer.

    B. An offeree makes the offer; an offeror receives the offer.

    C. A grantor makes the offer; a grantee receives the offer.

    D. A trustee makes the offer; a trustor receives the offer.

139. Which of the following is true regarding property dealings with minors?

    A. A minor may buy property and sell it.

    B. A minor may receive property as a gift and convey it.

    C. A minor may receive property as a gift but needs a guardian to sell it.

    D. A minor needs a guardian to inherit property and a guardian to sell it.

140. Who of the following would be least liable for misrepresentations made by the seller?

    A. the buyer's agent

    B. the seller's agent

    C. the seller's subagent

    D. all of the above, equally

141. What type of action is required to enforce a land contract?

    A. liability claim

    B. suit to quiet title

    C. eminent domain action

    D. condemnation suit

142. A safety clause in a listing agreement

    A. protects the seller against liability claims for injuries sustained by prospective buyers.

    B. guarantees the seller that the broker will use her best efforts to sell the property.

    C. guarantees that the seller will pay no commission if he sells the property without the assistance of the broker.

    D. guarantees that the broker will be paid under certain circumstances even if the listing agreement expires before the property is sold.

143. The requirement that a lease be in writing applies to all

    A. leases.
    B. residential leases.
    C. commercial leases.
    D. leases for longer than one year.

144. Rent payment in arrears means

    A. on the first day of each month.
    B. on the last day of each month.
    C. at the end of the lease term.
    D. on any agreed-upon date.

145. Tenant A subleases his apartment to Tenant B. Tenant A's interest is called a(n)

    A. assignment.
    B. novation.
    C. subleased fee.
    D. sandwich lease.

146. Which of the following is not a reason that a mobile home park tenancy may be terminated by the landlord?

    A. nonpayment of rent and utilities
    B. change of use of the park
    C. change in the number of occupants of the mobile home
    D. failure to comply with reasonable park rules

147. A retail store in a mall pays a base rent each month and a variable payment in addition to the base rent based on sales. This is most likely a(n)

    A. percentage lease.
    B. gross lease.
    C. indexed lease.
    D. graduated lease.

148. In a lease option, a portion of the rent

    A. must always be applied to the purchase price.
    B. may be applied to the purchase price.
    C. cannot be applied to the purchase price.
    D. is usually applied to pay for the option.

GO ON TO THE NEXT PAGE

149. One type of negotiable instrument is the

- **A.** deed of trust.
- **B.** promissory note.
- **C.** mortgage.
- **D.** hypothecation.

150. Buyer A agrees to make monthly payments to pay back the money he borrowed to purchase his home. Each payment will consist of principle and interest, every payment will be the same and the loan will be paid off with the last payment. He most likely signed a(n)

- **A.** straight note.
- **B.** hypothecated note.
- **C.** variable rate note.
- **D.** amortized note.

Answer Key for Practice Test 3

1. D	36. A	71. C
2. C	37. D	72. D
3. C	38. D	73. A
4. A	39. C	74. D
5. C	40. C	75. C
6. D	41. C	76. D
7. A	42. A	77. A
8. A	43. A	78. D
9. B	44. B	79. C
10. A	45. A	80. B
11. D	46. A	81. A
12. D	47. B	82. C
13. B	48. C	83. A
14. D	49. D	84. B
15. A	50. D	85. D
16. A	51. C	86. C
17. B	52. B	87. A
18. B	53. C	88. B
19. A	54. B	89. C
20. D	55. A	90. B
21. A	56. A	91. D
22. D	57. B	92. A
23. C	58. B	93. B
24. D	59. C	94. A
25. B	60. C	95. C
26. D	61. A	96. A
27. D	62. D	97. C
28. D	63. B	98. D
29. C	64. D	99. B
30. D	65. B	100. C
31. B	66. C	101. B
32. B	67. D	102. D
33. D	68. D	103. D
34. D	69. C	104. B
35. A	70. B	105. D

106. B

107. C

108. B

109. D

110. A

111. A

112. D

113. B

114. A

115. A

116. A

117. C

118. C

119. C

120. B

121. D

122. A

123. D

124. B

125. C

126. A

127. D

128. B

129. A

130. D

131. C

132. C

133. C

134. C

135. A

136. D

137. D

138. A

139. C

140. A

141. B

142. D

143. D

144. C

145. D

146. C

147. A

148. B

149. B

150. D

Answers and Explanations for Practice Test 3

1. **D.** The tricky answer choice here is personal property. A lease is considered personal property, not real estate.

2. **C.** The fluidity of gas and oil are acknowledged, but drilling underground to a neighbor's property is prohibited.

3. **C.** Because the stock is attached (appurtenant) to the land, the stock and the land must be transferred together.

4. **A.** Choices B, C, and D all deal with personal property. Fixtures are considered real property.

5. **C.** A section is a mile long on each side.

6. **D.** These lots were numbered and called government lots.

7. **A.** The law says that it must be filed in the county recorder's office for it to be used as a legal description.

8. **A.** Concurrent ownership refers to ownership by two or more people simultaneously.

9. **B.** Devisees and heirs are essentially the same thing. A person receiving real property through a will is called a devisee. A person receiving personal property through a will is called a legatee. Both are heirs in relationship to the estate of the decedent.

10. **A.** Given the facts of the question and absent any other information, this is separate property.

11. **D.** Tenancy in partnership requires equal, undivided interests in the real property. The real property in its entirety is made available to satisfy a partnership debt. Upon the death of one of the partners, the real property held by the partnership can pass to the surviving partner(s). What is not true is that the partnership interest in the real property would be subject to community property rules. Here there is a subtle line of distinction. Real property held in tenancy in partnership does not become community property upon the demise of one of the partners. However, the partnership itself may be subject to community property regulation.

12. **D.** An encumbrance can be physical or financial and may make transferring title difficult. It does not make title transfer impossible if someone is willing to acquire the property with the encumbrance.

13. **B.** The work may be planned or completed and notice of default must be provided.

14. **D.** This is an easement appurtenant. It is not a license, because the right has been given permanently.

15. **A.** Fair housing violations involve discrimination against protected classes.

16. **A.** This terminology emphasizes the fact that a buyer voluntarily agrees to these restrictions when he purchases the property.

17. **B.** The principle protection of a limited partnership is the limitation of liability to the partner's investment. This protection may be lost if the limited partner participates in the management of the company.

18. **B.** This is definitional. The wrong answer choices cover more specific issues than the general plan.

19. **A.** This is definitional.

20. **D.** Conditional use permits are for uses that may be specifically permitted but require additional review and control.

21. **A.** Individual building permits would normally be considered to have minimal environmental impact and, among the answer choices, would have the least environmental impact. This question also requires that you know that CEQA is the California Environmental Quality Act.

22. **D.** With respect to the conditional use permit, remember that, although it usually is a use listed in the zoning ordinance, it is a special use requiring special conditions.

23. **C.** The terms *grantor* and *grantee* are not usually used in association with a trust ownership situation.

24. **D.** The term *syndicate* is descriptive of a group of people pooling their funds to invest, but it is not a specific form of ownership or investment.

25. **B.** A partition action is used to dissolve a tenants-in-common situation when the owners cannot agree.

26. **D.** At least one of the interests in each of the other choices is an ownership interest.

27. D. In any problem like this, you can ignore the directions and concentrate on the fractions. You'll also have to remember that there are 640 acres in a section. So, $\frac{1}{2} \times \frac{1}{2} \times \frac{1}{4} \times 640$ acres = 40 acres.

28. D. The limit is $20,000 per transaction and $100,000 per licensee.

29. C. The broker needed to advise the seller of the whole deal and get her agreement in writing.

30. D. Choice C might confuse you, because most fees are paid this way, but other fee arrangements are possible and they are always negotiable.

31. B. The law says three business days.

32. B. This is the definition of inherent authority.

33. D. Client's funds must be kept separate from broker's own funds.

34. D. All agency agreements must be either initially in writing or confirmed in writing at some point.

35. A. In an open listing, a seller agrees (express) to pay a fee if the broker finds a buyer. The seller is under obligation to pay (unilateral) only if the broker finds a buyer. The broker is under no obligation to market the property or attempt to find a buyer.

36. A. The stated question is almost a classic definition of an employee from a tax perspective.

37. D. Cooperating brokers work with other brokers, but they work for whoever hires them.

38. D. Although most MLS organizations do not permit pocket listings, they are not inherently illegal or unethical.

39. C. If Choice D is confusing, remember that as long as an agent is paid according to the transactions she works on, she remains an independent contractor unless taxes and Social Security are withheld.

40. C. Remember that fiduciary duty may be given to the buyer, while the commission may be paid by either the buyer or the seller.

41. C. All we know for sure is that she is a cooperating broker, because cooperating brokers may be sellers' or buyers' agents and less likely dual agents.

42. A. For purposes of supervision, salespersons are always considered employees.

43. A. A listing agent must provide the disclosure before the listing agreement is signed. A buyer's agent must provide the disclosure to the buyer as soon as practical, but certainly before the buyer signs an offer to purchase. The disclosure form must again be presented to the seller before the offer is submitted and accepted by the seller. Choice A is the best choice here primarily because it is the obligation of the buyer's agent to present the agency disclosure form to the seller before presenting the offer and certainly before the seller signs acceptance of the offer. In those situations in which the buyer's agent does not directly present the offer to the seller, it is still the obligation of the buyer's agent to have the form prepared so that the listing agent can proceed in accordance with law.

44. B. The only close choice is D but the broker would not be breaking the law if the seller knew, so the word *always* makes this answer wrong.

45. A. The remaining activities listed in the choices require specific permission from the principal.

46. A. Potential gross income is an estimate of market income from all sources including rent, parking, vending, and laundry machines.

47. B. The cost approach is most useful for special-purpose or unique properties where there would be few comparables and no rental income.

48. C. This is a particularly difficult question because all the answers will likely have some effect on the value of the house. The fact that the question focuses on the relationship of the smaller homes to the larger one should lead you to the specific principle of regression.

49. D. An appraiser never adjusts the subject, so choices A and B can be eliminated. Then remember to ask yourself the question "What do I have to do to the comparable to make it like the subject?" In this case, because the comparable is better, you take away (subtract the value of) the feature.

50. D. Anticipation is an economic principle. The fourth characteristic of value is scarcity.

51. C. Spending money improving a property when there is no return on the expenditures is the definition of diminishing returns.

52. B. The method for finding this answer is to calculate how much per square foot the second house cost to build and then use that information to estimate the cost of the other house.

$338,000 ÷ 2,600 square feet = $130 per square foot

2,500 square feet × $130 = $325,000

Don't overthink this question by worrying about economies of scale (that is, that the 2,500-square-foot house would cost slightly more per square foot than the larger house to build). You really don't have enough information to account for that, and at only a 100-square-foot difference, that factor would be negligible or nonexistent.

53. C. *Functional utility* is generally defined as how well the design of a structure supports its use. Ultimately, the market will determine the usefulness or desirability of the design of a property and how well it meets the needs of the user.

54. B. Mortgage payments are never considered in the net operating income calculation because they relate more to the investor than to the building.

55. A. The historic cost index method, which uses a factor to account for increase in construction costs is most useful as a check on one of the other methods.

56. A. Choice B is wrong. Choices C and D may be semantically correct, but because the testers are interested in the licensee knowing the appropriate terms, the best choice is A.

57. B. The more houses you have on the market without an increase in the number of people who want those houses, the more likely prices are to go down.

58. B. You must read this question carefully, because it asks for the depreciated cost of the house not the amount of depreciation. Also, when a percent of depreciation is given, you must first multiply by that percentage and then subtract that amount from the reproduction/replacement cost.

Reproduction/Replacement Cost – Accrued Depreciation = Depreciated Cost

$200,000 – ($200,000 × 0.30) = $200,000 – $60,000 = $140,000

59. C. This type of problem involves increasing the value of the comparable by the amount of appreciation that has taken place.

$250,000 × 0.05 = $12,500

$250,000 + $12,500 = $262,500

60. C. Though not 100% true all the time, houses that sell in significantly less time than the average house and at a different ratio below the asking price than the average house have often been priced too low in the first place and, therefore, are not representative of market value.

61. A. Builders will often follow the success of other builders in an area (competition) until there is an oversupply of the space or dwelling units.

62. D. This question is tricky because market value is what appraisers are estimating *most* of the time—but not *all* the time. The value of something in exchange for something else is a more basic definition of value and, therefore, correct all the time.

63. B. Hopefully, you were able to eliminate choices A and C immediately. Anticipation often involves more predictable events. Change is a better fit for unpredictable natural and market events.

64. D. An acceleration clause allows the lender to declare the full loan due immediately under certain circumstances such as the buyer defaulting on the loan.

65. B. Given the circumstances where the broker actually provided some loan services to the buyer, a fee from the lender is legal.

66. C. The Federal Reserve System has no control over the other choices.

67. D. All the other choices are exemptions to the usury law.

68. D. A mortgage is a security instrument for a real estate loan but does not turn over title.

69. C. Joint and several liability means each owner can be required to pay the whole debt, regardless of shares owned or the type of title they have.

70. B. The real choice here involves understanding the antideficiency law, which would allow a deficiency judgment in this case.

71. C. The trustee holds title to the secured property for the benefit of the lender. If the debt is not paid, title may be conveyed to the beneficiary or the highest bidder at the trustee's sale.

72. D. Forgery is one of the defenses that may result in the note not being enforceable.

73. A. A deed in lieu of foreclosure transfers the property to the lender voluntarily without a foreclosure process.

74. D. Generally, PMI may be dropped when 25% of the home's value or mortgage amount has been paid off.

75. C. The buyer under these circumstances should require a contract contingency so that the contract can be cancelled.

76. D. RESPA affects federally related loans.

77. A. Regualtion Z takes effect at more than five units.

78. D. The opposite is true of each of the incorrect answers.

79. C. VA refinancing conditions include all the choices except using the money to purchase a second property.

80. B. The Federal Deposit Insurance Corporation (FDIC) insures deposits. It is not part of the secondary mortgage market.

81. A. The due-on-sale clause requires payment of the mortgage in full at the time of sale. There could be no wraparound mortgage in this case, because the original mortgage would have to be paid off.

82. C. After the debt is paid off, the trustee reconveys the deed back to the trustor.

83. A. Hypothecation is the pledging of property as security for a loan.

84. B. Choice C is wrong because "intestate" means there is no will.

85. D. The other answers are natural processes. A manmade addition is an improvement.

86. C. Owner A has acquired a right to use, not own, the property, without the permission of the neighbor.

87. A. The current owner who is the grantor (seller) was the buyer (grantee) at some point in the past.

88. B. The term *grant* in the grant deed implies certain warrantees.

89. C. This is definitional.

90. B. The demand for payoff is used if the loans are to be paid off.

91. D. This is definitional.

92. A. Because the oil was already paid for and will be purchased by the buyer, the seller is given a credit. Proration is the action of apportioning these costs.

93. B. Referral fees paid for title insurance businesses are illegal.

94. A. Because the buyer is the borrower, he usually pays for the lender's policy.

95. C. This time frame is statutory.

96. A. The tax lien is filed when the tax role for the following fiscal year is filed.

97. C. Deposit funds are returned to the buyer when an offer is not accepted.

98. D. Commingling, the mixing of the client's funds and the broker's funds, is never permitted.

99. B. This exception is permitted if the religious organization does not discriminate in its membership policies.

100. C. You should also know the meaning of the other terms. "Steering" is guiding people to or from certain neighborhoods, usually based on race, religion, or ethnicity. "Blockbusting" is using the prospect of a different racial or ethnic group moving into a neighborhood to scare people into selling. "Underwriting" is examining and approving information relative to a mortgage loan.

101. B. Because anyone looking at the property could readily determine for himself what the condition of the landscaping is, the broker is likely guilty of puffing or exaggerating but would not be liable for paying for new landscaping.

102. D. Blind advertising is illegal.

103. D. Three years from the listing date is acceptable only if the property didn't close.

104. B. State law requires a written agreement.

105. D. The law prohibits unlicensed assistants from dealing with clients.

106. B. This is the legal requirement with four members being unlicensed public members.

107. C. One year is the minimum time.

108. B. Offering a rebate to a prospective client is not a violation as long as the conditions for receiving the rebate are expressed with full disclosure to all parties and the offer is fulfilled.

109. D. In addition to choices A, B, and C, there are a number of other exemptions from the licensing requirements.

110. A. According to the Personal Responsibility and Work Opportunity Act of 1998, proof of legal presence in the United States must be presented to obtain or renew a real estate license.

111. A. The license is suspended until the licensee reimburses the fund.

112. D. In addition, Realtors may reveal confidential information in defending themselves when accused of wrongful conduct.

113. B. Disclosing the specific nature of the advertising to be done to market the property is not required.

114. A. The salesperson is an agent of the broker. Both can be Realtors. The broker is generally employed by the client as an independent contractor.

115. A. This is statutory.

116. A. This is statutory. Notice the wording in the question, "California requires"—the other state may require the broker to be licensed in that state as well.

117. C. An attorney in fact is one created by a power of attorney.

118. C. This is statutory.

119. C. This is statutory. Choice D might be disclosable if the park were to be located across the street or near the house.

120. B. This is statutory.

121. D. This is statutory.

122. A. You might think the answer to this is too simple, but normally a rental agreement would be executed when the buyer or seller is in possession of property to which he does not have title.

123. D. This is statutory.

124. B. This is statutory. The licensee's license will be suspended automatically when a payment is made from the account.

125. C. You never need a license to sell your own property.

126. A. An agency disclosure is only necessary if the homeowner is represented by a real estate broker.

127. D. This is statutory.

128. B. This is statutory.

129. A. This is statutory.

130. D. This is statutory.

131. C. Although the use of a mold disclosure statement is recommended, it is not mandatory; the other disclosures are.

132. C. I made this up.

133. C. This is essentially the definition of a voidable contract. The drunken party, once sober, can choose whether to go ahead with the deal or rescind the offer.

134. C. Leases for one year or less are the exception in the statute of frauds.

135. A. The term *discharge* is sometimes misunderstood as trying to break a contract in some way. A contract may be discharged by fulfilling all the terms of the contract and doing what was agreed to.

136. D. The agreement was implied because of the actions of the broker and the seller. Most listing agreements are unilateral. All real estate sales listing agreements must be in writing; therefore, this agreement is invalid.

137. D. The buyer-broker agreement should obtain the permission of the buyer to do this, or else a dual agency situation may arise.

138. A. This is definitional. Choices C and D do not apply to offers.

139. C. A minor may also inherit property directly, but a minor needs a guardian to convey title.

140. A. An argument might be made that, if the seller's agent and subagent were not aware of the misrepresentations, they might not be liable, but the least liable will be the buyer's agent.

141. B. This is statutory.

142. D. The safety clause guarantees that if, after the listing agreement expires, the seller sells the property to a buyer who was introduced by the broker to the seller, the broker will be paid the commission. A time frame after expiration of the listing agreement may be included in the listing contract as well as a requirement for the broker to provide a written list of names.

143. D. This is statutory.

144. C. *Arrears* means "after."

145. D. This is definitional.

146. C. This is statutory.

147. A. This is definitional. The additional payment is usually based on a percentage of gross sales.

148. B. Whether or not a portion of the rent is applied to the purchase price is negotiable.

149. B. The other answers have to do with security instruments rather than the promise to pay.

150. D. This is definitional.

Answer Sheet for Practice Test 4

(Remove This Sheet and Use It to Mark Your Answers)

1 Ⓐ Ⓑ Ⓒ Ⓓ	21 Ⓐ Ⓑ Ⓒ Ⓓ	41 Ⓐ Ⓑ Ⓒ Ⓓ	61 Ⓐ Ⓑ Ⓒ Ⓓ
2 Ⓐ Ⓑ Ⓒ Ⓓ	22 Ⓐ Ⓑ Ⓒ Ⓓ	42 Ⓐ Ⓑ Ⓒ Ⓓ	62 Ⓐ Ⓑ Ⓒ Ⓓ
3 Ⓐ Ⓑ Ⓒ Ⓓ	23 Ⓐ Ⓑ Ⓒ Ⓓ	43 Ⓐ Ⓑ Ⓒ Ⓓ	63 Ⓐ Ⓑ Ⓒ Ⓓ
4 Ⓐ Ⓑ Ⓒ Ⓓ	24 Ⓐ Ⓑ Ⓒ Ⓓ	44 Ⓐ Ⓑ Ⓒ Ⓓ	64 Ⓐ Ⓑ Ⓒ Ⓓ
5 Ⓐ Ⓑ Ⓒ Ⓓ	25 Ⓐ Ⓑ Ⓒ Ⓓ	45 Ⓐ Ⓑ Ⓒ Ⓓ	65 Ⓐ Ⓑ Ⓒ Ⓓ
6 Ⓐ Ⓑ Ⓒ Ⓓ	26 Ⓐ Ⓑ Ⓒ Ⓓ	46 Ⓐ Ⓑ Ⓒ Ⓓ	66 Ⓐ Ⓑ Ⓒ Ⓓ
7 Ⓐ Ⓑ Ⓒ Ⓓ	27 Ⓐ Ⓑ Ⓒ Ⓓ	47 Ⓐ Ⓑ Ⓒ Ⓓ	67 Ⓐ Ⓑ Ⓒ Ⓓ
8 Ⓐ Ⓑ Ⓒ Ⓓ	28 Ⓐ Ⓑ Ⓒ Ⓓ	48 Ⓐ Ⓑ Ⓒ Ⓓ	68 Ⓐ Ⓑ Ⓒ Ⓓ
9 Ⓐ Ⓑ Ⓒ Ⓓ	29 Ⓐ Ⓑ Ⓒ Ⓓ	49 Ⓐ Ⓑ Ⓒ Ⓓ	69 Ⓐ Ⓑ Ⓒ Ⓓ
10 Ⓐ Ⓑ Ⓒ Ⓓ	30 Ⓐ Ⓑ Ⓒ Ⓓ	50 Ⓐ Ⓑ Ⓒ Ⓓ	70 Ⓐ Ⓑ Ⓒ Ⓓ
11 Ⓐ Ⓑ Ⓒ Ⓓ	31 Ⓐ Ⓑ Ⓒ Ⓓ	51 Ⓐ Ⓑ Ⓒ Ⓓ	71 Ⓐ Ⓑ Ⓒ Ⓓ
12 Ⓐ Ⓑ Ⓒ Ⓓ	32 Ⓐ Ⓑ Ⓒ Ⓓ	52 Ⓐ Ⓑ Ⓒ Ⓓ	72 Ⓐ Ⓑ Ⓒ Ⓓ
13 Ⓐ Ⓑ Ⓒ Ⓓ	33 Ⓐ Ⓑ Ⓒ Ⓓ	53 Ⓐ Ⓑ Ⓒ Ⓓ	73 Ⓐ Ⓑ Ⓒ Ⓓ
14 Ⓐ Ⓑ Ⓒ Ⓓ	34 Ⓐ Ⓑ Ⓒ Ⓓ	54 Ⓐ Ⓑ Ⓒ Ⓓ	74 Ⓐ Ⓑ Ⓒ Ⓓ
15 Ⓐ Ⓑ Ⓒ Ⓓ	35 Ⓐ Ⓑ Ⓒ Ⓓ	55 Ⓐ Ⓑ Ⓒ Ⓓ	75 Ⓐ Ⓑ Ⓒ Ⓓ
16 Ⓐ Ⓑ Ⓒ Ⓓ	36 Ⓐ Ⓑ Ⓒ Ⓓ	56 Ⓐ Ⓑ Ⓒ Ⓓ	76 Ⓐ Ⓑ Ⓒ Ⓓ
17 Ⓐ Ⓑ Ⓒ Ⓓ	37 Ⓐ Ⓑ Ⓒ Ⓓ	57 Ⓐ Ⓑ Ⓒ Ⓓ	77 Ⓐ Ⓑ Ⓒ Ⓓ
18 Ⓐ Ⓑ Ⓒ Ⓓ	38 Ⓐ Ⓑ Ⓒ Ⓓ	58 Ⓐ Ⓑ Ⓒ Ⓓ	78 Ⓐ Ⓑ Ⓒ Ⓓ
19 Ⓐ Ⓑ Ⓒ Ⓓ	39 Ⓐ Ⓑ Ⓒ Ⓓ	59 Ⓐ Ⓑ Ⓒ Ⓓ	79 Ⓐ Ⓑ Ⓒ Ⓓ
20 Ⓐ Ⓑ Ⓒ Ⓓ	40 Ⓐ Ⓑ Ⓒ Ⓓ	60 Ⓐ Ⓑ Ⓒ Ⓓ	80 Ⓐ Ⓑ Ⓒ Ⓓ

81 Ⓐ Ⓑ Ⓒ Ⓓ	101 Ⓐ Ⓑ Ⓒ Ⓓ	121 Ⓐ Ⓑ Ⓒ Ⓓ	141 Ⓐ Ⓑ Ⓒ Ⓓ
82 Ⓐ Ⓑ Ⓒ Ⓓ	102 Ⓐ Ⓑ Ⓒ Ⓓ	122 Ⓐ Ⓑ Ⓒ Ⓓ	142 Ⓐ Ⓑ Ⓒ Ⓓ
83 Ⓐ Ⓑ Ⓒ Ⓓ	103 Ⓐ Ⓑ Ⓒ Ⓓ	123 Ⓐ Ⓑ Ⓒ Ⓓ	143 Ⓐ Ⓑ Ⓒ Ⓓ
84 Ⓐ Ⓑ Ⓒ Ⓓ	104 Ⓐ Ⓑ Ⓒ Ⓓ	124 Ⓐ Ⓑ Ⓒ Ⓓ	144 Ⓐ Ⓑ Ⓒ Ⓓ
85 Ⓐ Ⓑ Ⓒ Ⓓ	105 Ⓐ Ⓑ Ⓒ Ⓓ	125 Ⓐ Ⓑ Ⓒ Ⓓ	145 Ⓐ Ⓑ Ⓒ Ⓓ
86 Ⓐ Ⓑ Ⓒ Ⓓ	106 Ⓐ Ⓑ Ⓒ Ⓓ	126 Ⓐ Ⓑ Ⓒ Ⓓ	146 Ⓐ Ⓑ Ⓒ Ⓓ
87 Ⓐ Ⓑ Ⓒ Ⓓ	107 Ⓐ Ⓑ Ⓒ Ⓓ	127 Ⓐ Ⓑ Ⓒ Ⓓ	147 Ⓐ Ⓑ Ⓒ Ⓓ
88 Ⓐ Ⓑ Ⓒ Ⓓ	108 Ⓐ Ⓑ Ⓒ Ⓓ	128 Ⓐ Ⓑ Ⓒ Ⓓ	148 Ⓐ Ⓑ Ⓒ Ⓓ
89 Ⓐ Ⓑ Ⓒ Ⓓ	109 Ⓐ Ⓑ Ⓒ Ⓓ	129 Ⓐ Ⓑ Ⓒ Ⓓ	149 Ⓐ Ⓑ Ⓒ Ⓓ
90 Ⓐ Ⓑ Ⓒ Ⓓ	110 Ⓐ Ⓑ Ⓒ Ⓓ	130 Ⓐ Ⓑ Ⓒ Ⓓ	150 Ⓐ Ⓑ Ⓒ Ⓓ
91 Ⓐ Ⓑ Ⓒ Ⓓ	111 Ⓐ Ⓑ Ⓒ Ⓓ	131 Ⓐ Ⓑ Ⓒ Ⓓ	
92 Ⓐ Ⓑ Ⓒ Ⓓ	112 Ⓐ Ⓑ Ⓒ Ⓓ	132 Ⓐ Ⓑ Ⓒ Ⓓ	
93 Ⓐ Ⓑ Ⓒ Ⓓ	113 Ⓐ Ⓑ Ⓒ Ⓓ	133 Ⓐ Ⓑ Ⓒ Ⓓ	
94 Ⓐ Ⓑ Ⓒ Ⓓ	114 Ⓐ Ⓑ Ⓒ Ⓓ	134 Ⓐ Ⓑ Ⓒ Ⓓ	
95 Ⓐ Ⓑ Ⓒ Ⓓ	115 Ⓐ Ⓑ Ⓒ Ⓓ	135 Ⓐ Ⓑ Ⓒ Ⓓ	
96 Ⓐ Ⓑ Ⓒ Ⓓ	116 Ⓐ Ⓑ Ⓒ Ⓓ	136 Ⓐ Ⓑ Ⓒ Ⓓ	
97 Ⓐ Ⓑ Ⓒ Ⓓ	117 Ⓐ Ⓑ Ⓒ Ⓓ	137 Ⓐ Ⓑ Ⓒ Ⓓ	
98 Ⓐ Ⓑ Ⓒ Ⓓ	118 Ⓐ Ⓑ Ⓒ Ⓓ	138 Ⓐ Ⓑ Ⓒ Ⓓ	
99 Ⓐ Ⓑ Ⓒ Ⓓ	119 Ⓐ Ⓑ Ⓒ Ⓓ	139 Ⓐ Ⓑ Ⓒ Ⓓ	
100 Ⓐ Ⓑ Ⓒ Ⓓ	120 Ⓐ Ⓑ Ⓒ Ⓓ	140 Ⓐ Ⓑ Ⓒ Ⓓ	

Practice Test 4

Directions: For each of the following questions, select the choice that best answers the question.

1. Which pair of terms is most closely related?

   A. fee simple absolute and fee simple defeasible
   B. fee simple absolute and fee simple qualified
   C. fee simple qualified and fee simple defeasible
   D. fee simple absolute and life estate

2. Owner A allows B to use Owner A's property as long as C is alive. This is most likely

   A. a life estate.
   B. a lease.
   C. a fee simple conveyance.
   D. no transfer of any type of property.

3. Which of the following is true about ownership in severalty?

   A. It involves more than one person.
   B. It is a form of concurrent ownership.
   C. Another term for it is *sole ownership.*
   D. It is the same as fee simple absolute ownership.

4. The owner of a house wants to take his built-in bookcases with him when he sells the house. Which of the following is true?

   A. He can remove them because they are personal property.
   B. He should remove them and repair the wall before he offers the property for sale.
   C. He should remove them after the property is sold and repair the wall.
   D. He cannot remove them after they have been built in.

5. Cultivated crops are also called

   A. encumbrances.
   B. emblements.
   C. *fructus naturales.*
   D. fixtures.

6. If you purchased the northwest quarter of a section of land, what would the length of each side of the property be?

   A. 5,280 feet
   B. 2,640 feet
   C. 1,320 feet
   D. 660 feet

GO ON TO THE NEXT PAGE

7. Which of the following is most likely personal property in the context of a real estate transaction?

    A. window air conditioners

    B. a garden shed on a concrete foundation

    C. a fence

    D. a built-in microwave oven

8. Which of the following best describes riparian rights?

    A. the right of an owner to use lake water adjacent to her property

    B. the ownership by a landowner of the land underneath a navigable river adjacent to his land

    C. the ownership by a landowner of the land up to the high-water mark of a navigable river adjacent to his property

    D. the right of a landowner to use the water under his land

9. Owner A has a permanent right across Owner B's land to view the ocean. Owner B may not block that view. What might this be called with respect to Owner A?

    A. appurtenance

    B. emblement

    C. fee simple qualified

    D. fixture

10. The right of survivorship with respect to property owned by two or more people

    A. is an element of tenancy in common.

    B. is one of the benefits of ownership in severalty.

    C. requires a will to be effective.

    D. eliminates the probate process.

11. A husband dies and conveys his interest in a piece of real estate that was held as community property to his son from a previous marriage. The man's surviving wife and his son are now

    A. joint tenants.

    B. tenants in common.

    C. owners of community property.

    D. tenants in partnership.

12. A, B, and C pool their income to buy a multifamily house as an investment. Each of them takes on different management duties and can act on behalf of the group. Each also has full liability for the actions of any other member of the group. This arrangement is probably a(n)

    A. corporation.

    B. limited partnership.

    C. S corporation.

    D. general partnership.

13. When a person's land is rezoned to a use that reduces the value of the land by 25%, the owner

   A. is entitled to proportional compensation.
   B. is entitled to no compensation.
   C. has a claim under eminent domain law.
   D. can claim compensatory damages.

14. A property owner owns his house and the parcel of land it is built on. In addition, she has a common interest in the recreation areas, trails, and clubhouse. She most likely owns property in a

   A. planned unit development.
   B. condominium.
   C. cooperative.
   D. time-share.

15. Which of the following can a joint tenant not do?

   A. sell his interest in the property
   B. own an equal share of the property
   C. take title at the same time as the other owners
   D. will his share to his heirs

16. With respect to subdivided lands, which of the following is true?

   A. Sales may be closed before the final public report is issued.
   B. Sales may be closed when the conditional public report is issued.
   C. Reservations for future purchases may be taken when the conditional report is issued.
   D. Reservations for future sales may be taken before the conditional report is issued.

17. Renewal of a subdivision approval by the Real Estate Commissioner is available if all the lots have not been sold within

   A. two years.
   B. three years.
   C. four years.
   D. five years.

18. The local zoning ordinance permits lot coverage by all structures and impervious surfaces of 30%. How many square feet of a lot can be covered if the lot is 150 feet by 250 feet?

   A. 3,375 square feet
   B. 11,250 square feet
   C. 15,675 square feet
   D. 37,500 square feet

GO ON TO THE NEXT PAGE

19. The water table has to do with

    A. riparian rights.

    B. littoral rights.

    C. use of surface water.

    D. use of underground water.

20. A tenant in an apartment house attaches some bookcases to the wall. What is the presumption?

    A. that the bookcases are now a fixture and belong to the landlord

    B. that the bookcases are personal property and can be removed by the tenant

    C. that the bookcases are now real estate and can be removed only with the landlord's permission

    D. There is no presumption; their removal will have to be negotiated.

21. What is the number of the section that is always located in the northeast corner of a township?

    A. It is always different.

    B. 1

    C. 6

    D. 36

22. Which of the following provides special regulations for development along coastal area?

    A. Coastal Zone Conservation Act

    B. Oceans and Harbors Preservation Act

    C. Coastal Environment Preservation Act

    D. Coastal Beach Erosion Act

23. A commercial acre is best defined as the

    A. total acreage of the project.

    B. total acreage of the project divided by the number of individual lots.

    C. size of each development parcel.

    D. portion of an acre remaining after subtracting the area necessary for public improvements.

24. A township in the rectangular survey system always contains

    A. 640 acres.

    B. 1 square mile.

    C. 36 square miles.

    D. None of the above—it is not always the same area.

25. In joint tenancy, which unity deals with each party owning an equal share?

A. time
B. title
C. interest
D. possession

26. A subdivider plans on turning over the streets in a subdivision to the local town. This is most correctly called a

A. grant.
B. conveyance.
C. devise.
D. dedication.

27. A person who has a time-share

A. will always have an estate interest.
B. will always have a use interest.
C. will always have a use interest but never an estate interest.
D. can have an estate interest or a use interest but never both.

28. A real estate broker's services are used by a seller to locate a buyer. They discuss price, terms, and commissions, but no written agreement is signed. The broker is able to bring about a successful sale and sends a bill to the seller for his commission, which the seller refuses to pay. Which of the following is true?

A. The broker can enforce the commission claim because he brought about the sale.
B. The broker cannot enforce the commission claim because he has no written agreement.
C. The broker can enforce the commission claim through the State Recovery Fund.
D. The broker can enforce the commission claim if he can produce witnesses to the verbal agreement.

29. An offer by a listing broker to split a commission with a cooperating broker through the multiple listing system is an

A. express unilateral agreement.
B. express bilateral agreement.
C. implied unilateral agreement.
D. implied bilateral agreement.

30. Another term for implied agency is

A. unauthorized agency.
B. agency by ratification.
C. ostensible agency.
D. agency by estoppel.

GO ON TO THE NEXT PAGE

31. A broker negotiating a sale on behalf of a buyer when the buyer has not given him permission to do so is

    A. operating under implied authority.

    B. operating under apparent authority.

    C. operating under actual authority.

    D. simply being overly ambitious.

32. In addition to meeting all the legal requirements to establish an agency relationship, in order to collect a fee from someone for selling his house you must be

    A. a licensed real estate salesperson.

    B. a licensed real estate broker.

    C. acting gratuitously.

    D. none of the above

33. Broker A in representing Seller B lies to Buyer C about the condition of the property. Seller B knows that Broker A has lied but says nothing. Which of the following is true?

    A. Only the broker is liable to the buyer.

    B. Only the seller is liable to the buyer.

    C. The broker and seller will be liable to the buyer.

    D. There will be no liability because buyer beware supersedes disclosure.

34. A salesperson receives a deposit check as part of an offer on a house. She should

    A. give the check to her broker immediately.

    B. deposit the check into her escrow account.

    C. put the check in the file.

    D. cash the check but keep track of the money.

35. Which of the following would not be considered dual agency?

    A. two salespeople in the same company, one representing a buyer and one representing the seller for the same property

    B. a broker representing two different buyers who are interested in the same property as the buyers' agent

    C. a broker representing a buyer and seller for the same property

    D. a broker representing a seller as a client and a family member as a customer for the same house

36. Broker B is appointed by Broker A to help him sell a house. Broker A has permission from the seller to do this. Which of the following is true?

    A. Broker B is a subagent of Broker A.

    B. Broker B is a subagent of the seller.

    C. Broker B is an agent of Broker A.

    D. Broker B is an agent of the seller.

37. A broker who seeks to profit from a listing he has beyond his normal commission is violating the fiduciary principle of

A. loyalty.
B. confidentiality.
C. disclosure.
D. care.

38. Even upon request of the principal, a broker is not required to reveal which of the following information about the third party?

A. their financial condition
B. their current employment status
C. their race
D. their reason for buying the house

39. Based on an inspection of the property, which of the following is the selling broker responsible for knowing or finding out on behalf of a property purchaser?

A. information in public records
B. the location of the local town garbage collection facility 3 blocks away
C. deed restrictions prohibiting the operation of a home business on the property
D. evidence of water in the basement

40. A broker has an exclusive authorization and right-to-sell listing with a seller who wants $250,000 for her house. The broker decides to use his cousin to buy the house for himself at the full price because he knows he can resell it within a month for $300,000. Which of the following is true?

A. The broker would most likely be viewed as making a secret profit.
B. The broker could have accomplished this by revealing the whole situation to the seller.
C. The broker could have legally accomplished this with an option listing, provided he told the seller he was going to resell it at a higher price.
D. all of the above

41. For which of the following statements would a broker not likely be held liable in the sale of a $1,000,000 house?

A. "This house has a million-dollar view."
B. "This house will most likely sell for a million dollars in the next five years."
C. "This house is in the best school district in the state."
D. "You'll always be able to get your money back on this house."

42. A seller tells an agent that the furnace is 5 years old when in fact it is a well maintained 20-year-old furnace. The agent passes this information on to the buyer. When the truth is discovered by the purchaser after title closes, who will be held liable?

A. the owner and the broker
B. the owner but not the broker
C. the broker but not the owner
D. the purchaser for not having an inspection done

GO ON TO THE NEXT PAGE

43. Broker A, representing a seller, never conducted an inspection of the house, which would have revealed water damage in the basement. How long does the buyer have to sue the broker?

    A. one year

    B. two years

    C. five years

    D. The buyer cannot sue, because it was his responsibility to conduct the inspection.

44. Which of the following information should not be revealed when a broker is acting as a dual agent in a transaction?

    A. that the buyer will pay more than what she is offering

    B. that the home has a leaky roof

    C. that the buyer's financial condition may result in his not being approved for a mortgage loan

    D. that the seller needs an unusually long time before he can close on the house

45. Which of the following must be in a listing agreement to make a commission claim enforceable?

    A. permission to place the listing in MLS

    B. permission to put up a yard sign

    C. a definite termination date

    D. a reimbursement clause if the listing is terminated early

46. A nearby highway is being widened. You buy property along the highway because you expect property values to increase in the area. In making this investment, you are primarily using the principle of

    A. anticipation.

    B. competition.

    C. supply and demand.

    D. change.

47. A strip mall would most likely be appraised using the

    A. cost approach.

    B. income capitalization approach.

    C. gross rent multiplier approach.

    D. sales comparison approach.

48. If a home buyer is able to secure a private mortgage loan significantly below prevailing interest rates, what can the buyer afford to pay?

    A. more than another buyer with the same income

    B. less than another buyer with the same income

    C. the same as another buyer with the same income

    D. None of the above—interest rates have no impact on the buyer's purchasing power.

49. Which of the following statements about cost and value is true?

    A. They are always the same.
    B. They are never the same.
    C. They may be the same.
    D. The relationship is described by the principle of conformity.

50. The best definition of an appraisal is a(n)

    A. calculation of value.
    B. estimate of value.
    C. selection of value.
    D. analysis of value.

51. A four-bedroom house with only one bathroom is an example of

    A. functional obsolescence.
    B. physical deterioration.
    C. external obsolescence.
    D. none of the above

52. The potential additional value created by combining two adjacent lots is best described as

    A. change.
    B. anticipation.
    C. plottage.
    D. highest and best use.

53. The term *reconciliation* in appraising is best described as

    A. averaging the various values.
    B. weighted analysis of the various values.
    C. fitting one of the values to the sales price.
    D. estimating the value.

54. The subject property has three bathrooms. A comparable, similar in all respects to the subject property has two bathrooms and sold for $235,000. The value of the bathroom is estimated to be $15,000. What is the indicated value of the subject property?

    A. $250,000
    B. $235,000
    C. $220,000
    D. $205,000

GO ON TO THE NEXT PAGE

55. Potential gross income minus a vacancy and collection loss is

  A. scheduled income.
  B. net operating income.
  C. cash flow.
  D. effective gross income.

56. A vacant piece of land measuring 75 feet wide by 100 feet deep sells for $150,000. How much did it sell for per front foot?

  A. $2,000
  B. $1,500
  C. $200
  D. $20

57. Farmland is directly in the path of development. An appraisal would most likely find the current agricultural use to be

  A. the highest and best use.
  B. an interim use.
  C. a developmental use.
  D. an investment use.

58. The most probable price a well informed buyer would pay for a property that has been on the market for a reasonable period of time is a good definition of

  A. appraised value.
  B. investment value.
  C. market value.
  D. value in use.

59. What is the formula for calculating value using the income capitalization approach?

  A. Effective Gross Income ÷ Capitalization Rate = Value
  B. Gross Rent × Gross Rent Multiplier = Value
  C. Potential Gross Rent ÷ Capitalization Rate = Value
  D. Net Operating Income ÷ Capitalization Rate = Value

60. A separate estimate of the land value is part of which appraisal approach?

  A. sales comparison approach
  B. income capitalization approach
  C. gross rent multiplier approach
  D. cost approach

61. The comparables location is deemed to be 10% better than the subject location. The comparable recently sold for $350,000. What is the indicated value of the subject property?

    A. $365,000

    B. $350,000

    C. $315,000

    D. $300,000

62. In appraising a three-unit dwelling and wanting to analyze its income in the appraisal, what approach would you use?

    A. income capitalization approach

    B. gross rent multiplier approach

    C. sales comparison approach

    D. cost approach

63. A sale between family members in the sales comparison approach would require what type of adjustment?

    A. conditions of sale

    B. property rights

    C. financing concessions

    D. amenity adjustment

64. Which of the following is not one of the functions of the Federal Reserve System as a means of controlling the supply of money?

    A. to buy and sell government securities

    B. to set the discount rate

    C. to set reserve requirements

    D. to print money

65. A loan that does not qualify to be purchased by the federal secondary mortgage market is generally referred to as what type of loan?

    A. unconventional

    B. nonconventional

    C. subprime

    D. subsidized

66. In analyzing whether or not to approve a mortgage loan application, the lender will consider all but which of the following?

    A. the credit history of the borrower

    B. the ethnic background of the borrower

    C. the ability of the property to secure the debt

    D. the employment of the borrower

GO ON TO THE NEXT PAGE

67. Which of the following does not belong in the group?

A. Real Estate Settlement and Procedures Act
B. Consumer Credit Act
C. Truth in Lending Law
D. Regulation Z

68. Which of the following is not a requirement to be a holder in due course of a negotiable instrument? The instrument must have been taken

A. directly from the maker of the note.
B. for value.
C. in good faith.
D. without notice of it being overdue or any other defense.

69. The four-year statute of limitations with respect to a foreclosure applies to

A. judicial foreclosure only.
B. a trustee's sale only.
C. a default sale only.
D. all of the above

70. In the case of default on a loan secured by a trust deed, declaration of default is sent

A. by the beneficiary to the trustor.
B. by the trustee to the trustor.
C. by the beneficiary to the trustee.
D. by the trustee to the state controller.

71. What is the difference between buying property and assuming an existing mortgage or buying the property subject to an existing mortgage?

A. There is no difference.
B. The seller is still liable to the lender under the subject to situation.
C. The seller is still liable to the lender under the assumed mortgage situation.
D. The buyer is liable to the seller under the subject to situation.

72. What is a loan arranged by a builder that will pay off a construction loan and result in financing for the purchaser called?

A. wraparound loan
B. land contract
C. sale-leaseback
D. takeout loan

73. Which of the following agencies buys residential conventional mortgage loans?

    A. Office of Federal Housing Enterprise Oversight

    B. Federal Deposit Insurance Corporation

    C. Federal Home Loan Mortgage Corporation

    D. Office of Thrift Supervision

74. The commission that a mortgage loan broker may charge is determined by all of the following except

    A. the type of property mortgaged.

    B. whether it is secured by first or second deed of trust.

    C. the amount of the loan.

    D. the loan term.

75. A purchaser borrows $275,000 to purchase a property for a term of ten years. At the end of that time, $100,000 of the loan will have been paid off and the borrower will have to make a final payment of $175,000. What is the payment called?

    A. final payment

    B. balloon payment

    C. closing payment

    D. termination payment

76. A loan arrangement that allows payments to be made to a seller who, in turn, continues to make payments on an existing loan is called a(n)

    A. wraparound mortgage.

    B. wraparound trust deed.

    C. all-inclusive trust deed.

    D. all of the above

77. What is the government program that makes use of land contracts to transfer property to the buyer being assisted?

    A. FHA

    B. VA

    C. CAL-VET

    D. 203(b)

78. Which of the following are covered by Regulation Z rules?

    A. loans for business property

    B. loans for agricultural property

    C. loans for owner-occupied single-family houses

    D. loans for multifamily (six units or more) rental properties

GO ON TO THE NEXT PAGE

79. In a case where a borrower pays 2 discount points on a mortgage loan, which of the following is true?

A. The nominal rate and the APR will be the same.
B. The nominal rate will be lower than the APR.
C. The nominal rate will be higher than the APR.
D. The nominal rate will be higher than the APR but only in an adjustable-rate mortgage loan.

80. A buyer finances the purchase of a $280,000 house with a 100% financing. He must pay PMI until the LTV ratio reaches 75%. Assuming he pays off $10,000 per year on the loan and the house does not appreciate in value, at the end of how many years will he be able to drop the PMI?

A. 3
B. 5
C. 7
D. 8

81. Which of the following types of mortgage loans feature a monthly payment that does not change throughout the life of the loan?

A. fixed rate; fully amortized
B. fixed rate; partially amortized
C. graduated payment; fully amortized
D. growing equity; fully amortized

82. The guarantee made by the VA on a loan of 100% of the estimated value of the property will cost the borrower

A. nothing.
B. 1.5%.
C. 2.15%.
D. 3.0%.

83. Borrower A must pay 2½ points to secure a mortgage at the rate he wants. The value of the property is $390,000 and the LTV is 80%. How much does he owe the bank in points?

A. $9,750
B. $7,800
C. $6,240
D. $5,600

84. A testator wants to make a small change in her will. The way to do this is by adding a(n)

A. codicil.
B. amendment.
C. condition subsequent.
D. revision.

85. The sudden loss of land is called

    A. erosion.

    B. accretion.

    C. avulsion.

    D. reliction.

86. The state needs to build a road across Owner A's property. Owner A refuses to sell. The state could still obtain title to the property by exercising its right of

    A. succession.

    B. escheat. ·

    C. eminent domain.

    D. public grant.

87. Which of the following is not a requirement for a valid deed?

    A. acknowledgment

    B. grantor's signature

    C. delivery and acceptance

    D. granting clause

88. The trust deed, used as security for a debt is given by the

    A. trustee to the trustor on behalf of the beneficiary.

    B. trustor to the trustee on behalf of the beneficiary.

    C. trustor to the beneficiary on behalf of the trustee.

    D. beneficiary to the trustee on behalf of the trustor.

89. A deed of reconveyance is used to

    A. convey title to a purchaser after a foreclosure.

    B. return title to a trustor when the debt is paid.

    C. convey title after a tax sale.

    D. return title to the original owner after a title dispute.

90. What is the minimum surety bond requirement for an escrow agent?

    A. $5,000

    B. $10,000

    C. $25,000

    D. none

Practice Test 4

GO ON TO THE NEXT PAGE

91. In an escrow, closing title insurance is ordered by whom?

    A. the escrow agent

    B. the buyer

    C. the seller

    D. the real estate broker

92. Real estate taxes of $1,200 are due on a property on January 1 for the previous six months. Sale of the property closes on November 1. What is the proration?

    A. The buyer gets a credit of $800; the seller gets a debit of $400.

    B. The buyer gets a debit of $400; the seller gets a credit of $800.

    C. The buyer gets a credit of $400; the seller gets a debit of $800.

    D. The buyer gets a debit of $800; the seller gets a credit of $800.

93. The standard title insurance policy assumes that

    A. the property owner can inspect the property before he buys it.

    B. the property has no title defects.

    C. the property has a mortgage loan on the property.

    D. none of the above

94. The ALTA extended coverage policy protects against all of the following except

    A. mining claims.

    B. water rights.

    C. unrecorded easements or liens.

    D. zoning changes.

95. Which of the following types of property is not exempt from taxation?

    A. a church

    B. household furniture

    C. stocks

    D. a water treatment plant owned by Town A within the jurisdiction of Town B and built on the site of a former factory

96. Assuming that the tax collector takes the maximum legally allowed amount of time to sell a property for unpaid taxes, how long could the owner have to redeem it by paying the back taxes and penalties?

    A. three years

    B. five years

    C. seven years

    D. ten years

97. After an offer to purchase has been accepted, a broker should

    A. place the check in the file.

    B. deposit the check into his business account.

    C. deposit the check into a trust account.

    D. return the check to the buyer since the buyer will be submitting a larger check with the sales contract.

98. A broker's personal business funds may be placed in the trust he maintains

    A. never.

    B. to pay salaries.

    C. to pay expenses related to the sale.

    D. to pay service charges and fees to maintain the trust fund.

99. Buyer A sues Owner B for racial discrimination in an owner-occupied single-family house sale transaction, citing the 1866 Civil Rights Act. Owner B says he has an exemption under the 1968 Federal Fair Housing Act. What court case should Buyer A cite to prove Owner B wrong?

    A. *Jones v. Mayer*

    B. *Easton v. Strassburger*

    C. *United States v. Foley*

    D. None, because Owner B is correct.

100. Marital status is a protected class in the

    A. Federal Fair Housing Act of 1968.

    B. Unruh Civil Rights Act.

    C. Fair Employments and Housing Act.

    D. 1866 Civil Rights Act.

101. A broker selling a mobile home plans on advertising that no down payment will be required since he will direct a buyer to secure a loan for the down payment from a loan officer he does business with. Which of the following statements is correct about this situation?

    A. It is legal, as long as the broker receives no referral fee or other payment from the loan officer.

    B. It is legal, provided that, if the broker receives a referral payment from the loan officer, it is disclosed to the buyer.

    C. It is legal.

    D. It is illegal.

102. A broker making the statement "My kids went to this school district and we thought it was the best" to a prospective buyer is

    A. offering his opinion.

    B. puffing.

    C. falsely advertising.

    D. exaggerating.

GO ON TO THE NEXT PAGE

103. A broker must maintain transaction records

- A. for three years from the date of listing or three years from the date of closing, whichever is longer.
- B. for three years from the date of closing.
- C. for three years from the date of listing.
- D. until the broker closes the brokerage.

104. A broker is responsible for the actions of her salespersons

- A. always.
- B. only when they are employees.
- C. only when they are independent contractors.
- D. only when they have a written agreement.

105. An unlicensed assistant could

- A. service a real estate loan.
- B. solicit a listing.
- C. take photos of a prospective listing.
- D. meet with a homeowner to inspect the house.

106. By whom are the members of the Real Estate Advisory Commission appointed?

- A. the governor
- B. the real estate commissioner
- C. No one—they are elected.
- D. Half are appointed by the governor and half are appointed by the California Realtors Association.

107. What is the difference between suspension and revocation of a real estate license?

- A. There is no difference.
- B. Suspension is temporary; revocation is permanent.
- C. Revocation is temporary; suspension is permanent.
- D. The licensee can perform some real estate activities during suspension but not during revocation.

108. Which of the following could cause suspension or revocation of a real estate license?

- A. criminal activities resulting in conviction
- B. false advertising
- C. incompetence
- D. all of the above

109. Employees of a broker whose license has expired

- **A.** must stop working immediately.
- **B.** may continue to work until the broker renews her license.
- **C.** may work for 30 days.
- **D.** may work for 150 days.

110. How many hours of continuing education must a real estate licensee complete before renewing her license after the first four-year renewal period?

- **A.** 15 hours
- **B.** 25 hours
- **C.** 30 hours
- **D.** 45 hours

111. What is the maximum award that can be made from the Real Estate Recovery Account per transaction?

- **A.** $20,000
- **B.** $15,000
- **C.** $10,000
- **D.** $5,000

112. The purpose of a multiple listing service is to

- **A.** avoid dual agency.
- **B.** increase the potential to market the property by soliciting cooperating brokers.
- **C.** avoid the seller having to compensate buyers' agents.
- **D.** eliminate non-MLS members from selling a property.

113. Broker A lists a property for sale that he eventually becomes interested in buying. In order to satisfy the NAR code of ethics, he should

- **A.** walk away from the deal and not buy the property.
- **B.** have his wife or another relative buy the property.
- **C.** offer to pay for an appraisal of the property.
- **D.** disclose in writing to the owner that he is interested in buying the property.

114. All real estate brokers may call themselves

- **A.** Realtors.
- **B.** Realtists.
- **C.** real estate agents.
- **D.** any of the above

GO ON TO THE NEXT PAGE

Practice Test 4

115. An employee of a bank selling properties at foreclosure

    A. must have a salesperson's license.

    B. must have a broker's license.

    C. must obtain a temporary broker's license.

    D. is exempt from licensing requirements.

116. Under the regulations for operating a prepaid rental listing service license, what must a prospective tenant be provided with?

    A. at least three available rentals within five days of paying the fee

    B. at least five available rentals within three days of paying the fee

    C. at least ten available rentals within the first month of paying the fee

    D. There is no minimum requirement.

117. A commercial acre is

    A. 43,560 square feet.

    B. 40,000 square feet.

    C. the buildable area after setbacks are subtracted.

    D. the area remaining for development after streets, sidewalks, and other public dedications are subtracted.

118. An option to renew a lease is considered to be an option to

    A. both the landlord and the tenant.

    B. the tenant.

    C. the landlord.

    D. neither the tenant nor the landlord.

119. For purposes of disclosure, a material fact is best described as one that that involves

    A. the physical structure of the structure.

    B. factors involving the land on which the structure is built.

    C. publicly known issues affecting the neighborhood.

    D. facts that would affect the desirability or value of the property.

120. The obligation to inspect a property and disclose material defects to a third person includes

    A. direct, visually seen defects.

    B. evidence of physical problems that may require further investigation.

    C. any defect discoverable through a thorough inspection by the agent.

    D. all of the above

121. A seller removed a wall between two bedrooms to make it a larger room several years ago. This was a structural change to the house because of where the wall was located. What are his obligations to a buyer?

    A. none, because it was an alteration, not an addition

    B. to disclose the alteration only if it was not permitted

    C. to disclose the alteration and whether or not it was properly permitted

    D. to provide plans to the buyer so that the buyer may determine whether the alteration was structurally sound

122. The primary obligation of completing the Real Estate Disclosure Statement belongs to the

    A. broker.

    B. salesperson.

    C. owner.

    D. buyer.

123. Broker A has been found guilty of defrauding a number of people in a phony real estate investment scheme. The total losses to all victims of the fraud are $200,000. How much can they collect from the Recovery Account?

    A. $200,000

    B. $150,000

    C. $100,000

    D. $20,000 per victim, with no limit on the total amount

124. Seller A accepts Buyer B's offer to purchase her property. The next day she delivers the completed Transfer Disclosure Statement to the buyer. How many days does the buyer have to rescind the offer to purchase?

    A. none, because the offer was already accepted

    B. seven

    C. five

    D. three

125. The use of a fictitious name for a brokerage is

    A. legal.

    B. commonly known as a *doing business as* (DBA).

    C. legal if filed with the county clerk.

    D. all of the above

126. Which of the following activities could be performed without a real estate license?

    A. collecting rents for several owners of apartment buildings

    B. conducting a preliminary interview with a prospective home-selling client

    C. accompanying the appraiser on her inspection of the property that is being sold

    D. negotiating a mortgage loan

GO ON TO THE NEXT PAGE

127. When a salesperson changes her affiliation with a broker, how many days do she and the new broker have to notify the state?

A. two
B. three
C. five
D. seven

128. For an environmental hazard to be required to be disclosed, it must

A. be located on or near the property.
B. potentially affect the property.
C. specifically be known to the seller or agent.
D. all of the above

129. The seller's broker invites the cooperating broker who sold the property to join her on a visit to inspect the property. The cooperating broker indicates that he doesn't need to inspect the property, because the seller's broker is already performing that task. The cooperating broker

A. is correct.
B. is wrong.
C. is correct if the house is anything except a one-family house.
D. must inspect the property but need not report his findings to anyone but the seller's broker.

130. According to the lead-based paint disclosure law, how many days must a buyer be given to have the house tested for lead-based paint hazard?

A. five
B. ten
C. 15
D. 20

131. The law that governs development in earthquake-prone areas and also requires seller disclosure of this information is the

A. Seismic Hazards Mapping Act.
B. Earthquake Fault Zone Development and Notification Act.
C. Earthquake Zone Development Management Act.
D. Alquist-Priolo Earthquake Fault Zoning Act.

132. Mold disclosure is best covered by using

A. the Real Estate Transfer Disclosure Statement.
B. the Natural Hazard Disclosure Statement.
C. the environmental condition assessment report.
D. a mold disclosure form.

133. Buyer A signs an agreement to purchase Seller B's house. Buyer A must obtain financing before proceeding with the purchase. The contract could be described as

    A. void.
    B. voidable.
    C. executed.
    D. executory.

134. Homeowner A puts a sign in front of his property after a snowstorm that says he will pay $25 to anyone shoveling his driveway. What kind of contract has he created?

    A. express unilateral
    B. express bilateral
    C. implied unilateral
    D. implied bilateral

135. After a property purchase agreement is signed, a survey is done and a mistake is discovered in the size of the lot. A survey is done noting that the property is smaller than originally described. Because the purchaser wants to go ahead with the purchase, he would likely seek a(n)

    A. assignment.
    B. rescission.
    C. reformation.
    D. release.

136. The law that requires most real estate contracts to be in writing is called the

    A. Parol Evidence Law.
    B. Truth in Lending Law.
    C. Statute of Frauds.
    D. Real Estate Settlement and Procedures Act.

137. A buyer's agency agreement must state that

    A. the buyer agrees to a dual agency.
    B. all commissions are negotiable.
    C. the seller must pay the commission.
    D. the buyer must pay the commission.

138. An offer to purchase property made by a person under the influence of alcohol is best described as

    A. voidable.
    B. void.
    C. unenforceable.
    D. valid.

GO ON TO THE NEXT PAGE

139. An offer to purchase real estate is revocable by

    A.   the person making the offer.

    B.   the person receiving the offer.

    C.   the person making the offer, as long as the offer is not in writing.

    D.   the person making the offer, as long as no money accompanies the offer.

140. If the terms of a contract are illusory, they are

    A.   valid.

    B.   certain.

    C.   uncertain.

    D.   clear.

141. A listing agreement is generally

    A.   express and executed.

    B.   express and executory.

    C.   express and unilateral.

    D.   implied and executory.

142. A listing agreement establishes a relationship between

    A.   buyer and seller.

    B.   seller and broker.

    C.   seller and salesperson.

    D.   broker and salesperson.

143. The type of leasehold estate that has a definite termination date is called an

    A.   estate for years.

    B.   estate at sufferance.

    C.   estate at will.

    D.   estate from period to period.

144. Automatic renewal of a lease may be voidable if the

    A.   renewal clause is not printed in the correct size type.

    B.   renewal clause is not located in the correct place in the lease.

    C.   lease is for a year and was not in writing.

    D.   all of the above

145. The opposite of untenantable is

    A. livable.
    B. unlivable.
    C. actual eviction.
    D. tenancy at sufferance.

146. An escalator clause relates to

    A. maintenance issues in a lease.
    B. adjustments in mortgage rates in adjustable-rate mortgages.
    C. rental rate adjustments based on an index.
    D. percentage adjustments in a percentage lease.

147. A homeowner in a mobile home park has defaulted on his bills, such as rent and utilities, a number of times. Each time he manages to pay the bills within the prescribed time period after the notice of termination. What is that time period?

    A. three days
    B. seven days
    C. 21 days
    D. 30 days

148. Which of the following actions would not be considered a rejection of an offer to purchase a property?

    A. ignoring the offer
    B. rejecting the offer in writing
    C. making a counteroffer
    D. revoking the offer by the buyer

149. The offer of pledging of real property to secure a loan is called a(n)

    A. promissory note.
    B. hypothecation.
    C. negotiable instrument.
    D. due on sale clause.

150. Buyer A promises to pay off all the interest on the loan he used to buy the property in monthly installments and pay off the principal with the last payment of interest. He most likely signed a(n)

    A. straight note.
    B. installment note.
    C. amortized note.
    D. adjustable rate note.

Answer Key for Practice Test 4

1. C	36. B	71. B
2. A	37. A	72. D
3. C	38. C	73. C
4. B	39. D	74. A
5. B	40. D	75. B
6. B	41. A	76. D
7. A	42. B	77. C
8. C	43. B	78. C
9. A	44. A	79. B
10. D	45. C	80. C
11. B	46. A	81. A
12. D	47. B	82. C
13. B	48. A	83. B
14. A	49. C	84. A
15. D	50. B	85. C
16. C	51. A	86. C
17. D	52. C	87. A
18. B	53. B	88. B
19. D	54. A	89. B
20. B	55. D	90. C
21. B	56. A	91. A
22. A	57. B	92. C
23. D	58. C	93. A
24. C	59. D	94. D
25. C	60. D	95. D
26. D	61. C	96. C
27. B	62. B	97. C
28. B	63. A	98. D
29. A	64. D	99. A
30. C	65. C	100. C
31. B	66. B	101. D
32. B	67. A	102. A
33. C	68. A	103. A
34. A	69. A	104. A
35. B	70. C	105. C

106. B	**121.** C	**136.** C
107. B	**122.** C	**137.** B
108. D	**123.** C	**138.** A
109. A	**124.** D	**139.** A
110. D	**125.** D	**140.** C
111. A	**126.** C	**141.** B
112. B	**127.** C	**142.** B
113. D	**128.** D	**143.** A
114. C	**129.** B	**144.** D
115. D	**130.** B	**145.** A
116. A	**131.** D	**146.** C
117. D	**132.** D	**147.** D
118. B	**133.** D	**148.** D
119. D	**134.** A	**149.** B
120. D	**135.** C	**150.** A

Answers and Explanations for Practice Test 4

1. C. Both these terms refer to the fact that there is a condition with respect to the use of the property that could cause a loss of ownership.

2. A. A life estate can be for the lifetime of the holder of the life estate or another person.

3. C. Choice D might appear correct, except ownership in severalty could be fee simple qualified if there is a condition on the ownership.

4. B. Logically, a homeowner can do pretty much anything within building code and zoning code laws before he offers his house for sale.

5. B. *Fructus naturales* are naturally growing plants as opposed to cultivated crops.

6. B. A section is a square that is 1 mile long on each side. Because there are four quarters in each section, each quarter-section measures ½ mile or 2,640 feet (1 mile = 5,280 feet) on each side.

7. A. The fact that the items in the three incorrect answer choices are permanently attached to the ground or the structure make them all fixtures.

8. C. Riparian rights have to do with flowing water (rivers and streams), and the rights of the adjacent landowner depend on whether or not the river or stream is navigable.

9. A. An appurtenance is anything (usually a right) that attaches to the land for the benefit of the landowner. Do not confuse this with a fixture, which is a physical thing attached to the land.

10. D. The right of survivorship allows the deceased person's share to go to the other owner(s) without probate or the need for a will.

11. B. In the situation described, the new owner (the son) becomes a tenant in common with the wife.

12. D. The description most closely resembles the characteristics of a general partnership.

13. B. Normally, a person is entitled to compensation only when the all reasonable use of the property has been denied.

14. A. The primary distinction here is between a condominium and a planned unit development. The condominium owner owns the air space of her unit and has a common interest in the land.

15. D. One of the important distinguishing factors of joint tenancy is that the owner cannot will his share to an heir.

16. C. No sales may be closed until the final report is received.

17. D. This is statutory and part of the Subdivided Lands Law.

18. B. The word *impervious* means areas including driveways through which rainwater can't drain. First, you have to calculate the area of the parcel; then you take 30% of that area. Here's the math:

Length × Width = Area

250 feet × 150 feet = 37,500 square feet

37,500 square feet × 0.30 = 11,250 square feet

19. D. The water table is the distance from the surface of the ground to a depth at which natural groundwater is found.

20. B. In general, the view is that the bookcases still belong to the tenant.

21. B. You don't need a map for this. Just remember that sections within a township are always numbered by starting in the top row on the right (northeast corner) with the number 1 and going left from there.

22. A. The wrong answer choices are all made up.

23. D. This is definitional.

24. C. Don't get confused with the area of a section, which is 640 acres or 1 square mile.

25. C. This is definitional.

26. D. Although all the terms imply some form of transfer of ownership of property, the correct term for this type of conveyance in connection with a subdivision is *dedication*.

27. B. It is the nature of timeshare ownership to permit use of the property for a period of time. The estate or ownership interest varies.

28. B. Agency agreements must be in writing for a commission claim to be enforced.

29. A. The broker has stated (express) that she will share the commission if (unilateral) another broker finds a buyer. The other brokers are under no obligation to act.

30. C. This is definitional.

31. B. Apparent authority gives the false impression that an agency relationship exists.

32. B. You might argue that choices A and B are both correct, but remember that a salesperson cannot collect a fee from someone other than his broker. *Gratuitously* means for free, so no fee is involved.

33. C. The point of this question is that the seller's silence creates liability for the seller.

34. A. The check might be put in a file (Choice C) until the offer is accepted, but the better action is to give the check to the broker and follow his instructions.

35. B. Nothing in license law precludes the broker from representing two buyers for the same property, although the fact that two buyers represented by the same broker may be competing for the same property is usually disclosed. Choice D may be a little tricky, but most people would assume that a broker working with a family member even as a customer would tend to represent the family member's interest, creating, in this case, a possible undisclosed dual agency.

36. B. The key here is that the seller (the principal) gave permission. If no permission had been given, Broker B would have been an agent of Broker A.

37. A. The principle of loyalty says that the broker must put his principal's interest above all others, even his own.

38. C. Issues of race, creed, or color are not considered material facts and should not be disclosed even if requested.

39. D. The other items could be revealed but are not required as a result of the required visual inspection of the property by the broker.

40. D. All of the statements concerning secret profit are true.

41. A. This statement is clearly an expression of the quality of the view and is easily verifiable by the buyer. The other statements are much more specific and depend on future events, which, if they do not come to pass, could result in liability on the part of the broker.

42. B. As long as the broker was repeating information that could not be verified by a physical inspection, only the owner would be held liable.

43. B. The broker should have inspected the property, and the buyer has two years in which to sue.

44. A. The other choices are material facts that not only need not be kept confidential but would most likely fall under disclosure requirements.

45. C. All the other choices are optional. Reimbursement has to do with expenses if the listing is terminated before sale of the property.

46. A. This question is difficult because all of the answer choices fit in some way, but first and, therefore, primarily you are anticipating that property values will rise because of the highway improvement.

47. B. The income capitalization approach is used to appraise income producing properties, including commercial property, as well as large-scale residential investment property.

48. A. The buyer's purchasing power is extended by the lower interest rate.

49. C. You might be tempted to select Choice D, unless you know what conformity means.

50. B. Although appraisers do many calculations, perform significant analysis of the market, and select comparables and other information, an appraisal is defined as an estimate or opinion of value.

51. A. Functional obsolescence is a design feature that does not meet current standards for the particular use.

52. C. The other answers may have a bearing on the ultimate value of the property, but plottage refers to the specific value change due to the joining of two smaller lots to make a larger one.

53. B. Reconciliation is the process by which appraisers analyze the values arrived at through the three appraisal methods and then give each of them appropriate weight in order to arrive at a final value conclusion. The three values are never averaged to come up with a final value.

54. A. If the comparable is worse than the subject, you add the value of the feature to the sale price of the comparable.

$235,000 + $15,000 = $250,000

55. D. The second step in reconstructing an income and expense statement is to subtract the vacancy and collection loss from potential gross income to arrive at effective gross income.

56. A. Frontage is usually the width across the front of a property along the road. Price per front foot is found by dividing the total cost of the property by the number of front feet.

$150,000 ÷ 75 feet = $2,000 per front foot

57. B. Choices C and D may have some meaning as descriptive terms but have no specific definition with respect to analyzing highest and best use. An interim use is one that is temporary in light of future development.

58. C. This is the usual wording in a definition of market value. Remember that an appraisal sometimes is done for some value other than market value.

59. D. The income capitalization approach uses the net operating income to calculate value.

60. D. The only approach that requires a separate land value is the cost approach.

61. C. The buyers already paid 10% more to live in the comparable's neighborhood. What would they have paid to live in the subject neighborhood? The answer is 10% less, so 10% is subtracted from the sale price of the comparable.

$350,000 × 0.10 = $35,000

$350,000 − $35,000 = $315,000

62. B. The income approach is used for large-scale income producing properties like shopping malls. Choices C and D do not take income into account.

63. A. Sales that may not be true reflections of market value transactions—such as sales between family members, foreclosure sales, and sales under extreme duress—may require an adjustment for conditions of sale.

64. D. The Treasury Department is responsible for printing money.

65. C. *Subprime* is the term used for these loans.

66. B. Credit applicants are protected from discrimination by the Equal Credit Opportunity Act (ECOA).

67. A. Although RESPA deals with consumer protection in the credit process, choices B, C, and D are all names for essentially the same law.

68. A. Choices B, C, and D are the statutory requirements to be a holder in due course.

69. A. There really is no such thing as a default sale except as the term might be used to describe any sale resulting from defaulting on a loan.

70. C. The declaration of default is the first step in the process and goes from the beneficiary (the lender) to the trustee (the third party holding the deed of trust).

71. B. "Subject to" does not relieve the seller of liability for the mortgage debt in the event that the buyer defaults.

72. D. This is definitional.

73. C. This agency, known as Freddie Mac, is part of the secondary mortgage market.

74. A. The type of property that is being mortgaged doesn't matter.

75. B. Though the other answers may be somewhat descriptive, the final payment is called a balloon payment.

76. D. When generally talking about loans, the terms *mortgage* and *trust deed* mean the same thing. Choices A, B, and C are names for the same type of loan arrangement.

77. C. The Cal-Vet loan purchases the property and sells it to the qualified veteran using a land contract.

78. C. The regulation is generally designed to protect home buyers.

79. B. Discount points are prepaid interest and will result in a lower nominal rate and higher APR.

80. C. Because there is no appreciation on the value of the property, the loan-to-value ratio (LTV) will reach 75% when the owner pays off 25% of the mortgage loan.

$280,000 × 0.25 = $70,000

$70,000 ÷ $10,000 per year payoff = 7 years

81. A. The tricky answer choice is B. If the loan is not fully amortized, then the remaining balance is due at the last payment, which means all the payments are not the same.

82. C. The current fee is 2.15% of the loan amount.

83. B. The key thing to remember is that a point is 1% of the loan amount, not 1% of the value or cost of the property.

$390,000 (Value of Property) × 0.80 (Loan-to-Value Ratio) = $312,000 (Amount of Mortgage Loan)

$312,000 (Loan value) × 0.025 (Points) = $7,800

84. A. Choices B and D could be viewed as generic terms for any type of change in a document, but the proper term for a change in a will without writing a new will is a codicil. Choice C refers to deeds.

85. C. Erosion is the gradual loss of surface soil.

86. C. The state, through a suit of condemnation, acquires title by using its right of eminent domain.

87. A. The acknowledgment is necessary to record the deed but is not necessary to make it valid.

88. B. This is definitional as to how a trust deed works.

89. B. This is definitional.

90. C. The law requires a $25,000 surety bond.

91. A. Choice A is clearly the correct answer even though a real estate broker may act as an escrow agent.

92. C. The buyer will be paying the taxes in arrears but not living in the house for the entire six months, so the seller will owe the buyer for the portion of time the seller is in the house. The buyer gets a credit and the seller gets a debit.

$1,200 ÷ 6 months = $200 per month

$200 per month × 4 months (Time Period Seller Was in the House for Which the Buyer Paid the Taxes) = $800 credit to buyer

Because the buyer paid for the taxes the seller "used," the seller is charged a debit for the same amount.

93. A. The standard policy assumes that the owner by inspection of the property will discover obvious defects or other claims, such as easements against the title.

94. D. Zoning changes are normally not covered in standard or extended coverage policies.

95. D. Generally, municipally owned property is exempt, but under special circumstances it is taxable if it's in another jurisdiction.

96. C. The owner has five years to redeem the property, during which time the tax collector cannot sell it, and the tax collector has two years after that to sell it, during which time it can still be redeemed.

97. C. Deposit funds are placed in the broker's trust account after the offer has been accepted.

98. D. This is one of two exceptions to the no commingling rule.

99. A. This case upheld the Civil Rights Act of 1866 that prohibited racial discrimination in all property transactions.

100. C. The other laws do not include marital status as a protected class.

101. D. This situation as stated in the question is prohibited.

102. A. Clearly this is an opinion.

103. A. Note that, technically, choices B and C could be correct but Choice A is the most complete and, therefore, the best answer.

104. A. Arguably, Choice B could also be correct because all salespersons are treated as employees for supervision purposes, but Choice A is a better choice because it provides for no exceptions.

105. C. The photos would be considered primarily a clerical or administrative type of function, which is generally what an unlicensed assistant is permitted to do.

106. B. The commissioner appoints the members.

107. B. A suspended license will generally be reinstated automatically at the end of the suspension period. A revoked license would require reapplication.

108. D. As a matter of exam preparation as well as eventual real estate practice, you should familiarize yourself with all the actions that may result in a temporary or permanent loss of your real estate license.

109. A. Because a salesperson must always work under a broker's supervision, if the broker's license lapses for any reason, the salesperson must stop working until the broker's license is reactivated or affiliate with another broker.

110. D. This is statutory.

111. A. This is statutory.

112. B. This is definitional.

113. D. Article 4-1 requires this.

114. C. You must be a member of the appropriate organization in order to call yourself anything but Choice C.

115. D. This is statutory.

116. A. This is statutory.

117. D. This is definitional.

118. B. An option is one party's right and the other party's obligation. A landlord cannot force a tenant to remain.

119. D. You could correctly argue that the other three answer choices are material facts, but they are too limited because a material fact is anything that would affect the desirability of the property and, therefore, the buyer's decision.

120. D. This is statutory.

121. C. This is statutory.

122. C. Although a portion of the statement is to be completed by the brokers involved, the primary responsibility is the owner's.

123. C. This is statutory.

124. D. It is three because it was delivered. It would be five if mailed.

125. D. This is statutory.

126. C. All the other activities by law require a real estate license.

127. C. This is statutory.

128. D. The environmental hazard must be known to exist, and it must either be on the property or, if near the property, have or could have an effect on the property.

129. B. The cooperating broker must inspect the property and complete the inspection disclosure form that is given to the buyer.

130. B. This is statutory.

131. D. Choice A governs seismic hazards. I made up choices B and C.

132. D. Although this is not mandatory, it is recommended and it is the best way to disclose the condition. I made up Choice C. It should be noted that mold, as a possible environmental hazard, should most likely be noted on the property disclosure transfer form.

133. D. When describing a contract, the term *executory* means that the contract has been made but that there are some conditions that must be met and that the final goal (in this case, the sale of the property) has not yet occurred.

134. A. Homeowner A has expressed his willingness to pay for the shoveling. He is obligated to pay, but no one is obligated to shovel.

135. C. In contract terminology, the term *reformation* means to correct some error in a contract.

136. C. This is statutory.

137. B. The other answers are often mentioned in a buyer's agency agreement but the only mandatory notice is the one about all broker fees being negotiable.

138. A. The contract may appear to be unenforceable or void, but, technically, when the person is sober, he can affirm the contract and go ahead with the deal or he can decide to void it.

139. A. A normal offer to purchase—even if accompanied by so-called good faith or earnest money—is revocable until accepted and a meeting of the minds is achieved.

140. C. The term *illusory* indicates that the terms may be uncertain.

141. B. The terms of the agreement have not been completed fulfilled, so it is executory; because it is in writing, it is express. The word *generally* is there because, although a listing agreement could be implied, collecting the commission would be unenforceable.

142. B. A listing agreement may name a salesperson as having acquired the listing, but the agreement itself establishes the relationship between the broker and the seller.

143. A. A definite termination date characterizes the estate for years.

144. D. All of these are statutory provisions.

145. A. The terms *tenantable* and *untenantable* are equivalent to *livable* and *unlivable* and usually refer to the possibility of constructive eviction.

146. C. This is definitional.

147. D. This is statutory.

148. D. All the other answers are ways in which an offer may be rejected.

149. B. This is definitional.

150. A. This is definitional.

Answer Sheet for Practice Test 5

(Remove This Sheet and Use It to Mark Your Answers)

1 Ⓐ Ⓑ Ⓒ Ⓓ	21 Ⓐ Ⓑ Ⓒ Ⓓ	41 Ⓐ Ⓑ Ⓒ Ⓓ	61 Ⓐ Ⓑ Ⓒ Ⓓ
2 Ⓐ Ⓑ Ⓒ Ⓓ	22 Ⓐ Ⓑ Ⓒ Ⓓ	42 Ⓐ Ⓑ Ⓒ Ⓓ	62 Ⓐ Ⓑ Ⓒ Ⓓ
3 Ⓐ Ⓑ Ⓒ Ⓓ	23 Ⓐ Ⓑ Ⓒ Ⓓ	43 Ⓐ Ⓑ Ⓒ Ⓓ	63 Ⓐ Ⓑ Ⓒ Ⓓ
4 Ⓐ Ⓑ Ⓒ Ⓓ	24 Ⓐ Ⓑ Ⓒ Ⓓ	44 Ⓐ Ⓑ Ⓒ Ⓓ	64 Ⓐ Ⓑ Ⓒ Ⓓ
5 Ⓐ Ⓑ Ⓒ Ⓓ	25 Ⓐ Ⓑ Ⓒ Ⓓ	45 Ⓐ Ⓑ Ⓒ Ⓓ	65 Ⓐ Ⓑ Ⓒ Ⓓ
6 Ⓐ Ⓑ Ⓒ Ⓓ	26 Ⓐ Ⓑ Ⓒ Ⓓ	46 Ⓐ Ⓑ Ⓒ Ⓓ	66 Ⓐ Ⓑ Ⓒ Ⓓ
7 Ⓐ Ⓑ Ⓒ Ⓓ	27 Ⓐ Ⓑ Ⓒ Ⓓ	47 Ⓐ Ⓑ Ⓒ Ⓓ	67 Ⓐ Ⓑ Ⓒ Ⓓ
8 Ⓐ Ⓑ Ⓒ Ⓓ	28 Ⓐ Ⓑ Ⓒ Ⓓ	48 Ⓐ Ⓑ Ⓒ Ⓓ	68 Ⓐ Ⓑ Ⓒ Ⓓ
9 Ⓐ Ⓑ Ⓒ Ⓓ	29 Ⓐ Ⓑ Ⓒ Ⓓ	49 Ⓐ Ⓑ Ⓒ Ⓓ	69 Ⓐ Ⓑ Ⓒ Ⓓ
10 Ⓐ Ⓑ Ⓒ Ⓓ	30 Ⓐ Ⓑ Ⓒ Ⓓ	50 Ⓐ Ⓑ Ⓒ Ⓓ	70 Ⓐ Ⓑ Ⓒ Ⓓ
11 Ⓐ Ⓑ Ⓒ Ⓓ	31 Ⓐ Ⓑ Ⓒ Ⓓ	51 Ⓐ Ⓑ Ⓒ Ⓓ	71 Ⓐ Ⓑ Ⓒ Ⓓ
12 Ⓐ Ⓑ Ⓒ Ⓓ	32 Ⓐ Ⓑ Ⓒ Ⓓ	52 Ⓐ Ⓑ Ⓒ Ⓓ	72 Ⓐ Ⓑ Ⓒ Ⓓ
13 Ⓐ Ⓑ Ⓒ Ⓓ	33 Ⓐ Ⓑ Ⓒ Ⓓ	53 Ⓐ Ⓑ Ⓒ Ⓓ	73 Ⓐ Ⓑ Ⓒ Ⓓ
14 Ⓐ Ⓑ Ⓒ Ⓓ	34 Ⓐ Ⓑ Ⓒ Ⓓ	54 Ⓐ Ⓑ Ⓒ Ⓓ	74 Ⓐ Ⓑ Ⓒ Ⓓ
15 Ⓐ Ⓑ Ⓒ Ⓓ	35 Ⓐ Ⓑ Ⓒ Ⓓ	55 Ⓐ Ⓑ Ⓒ Ⓓ	75 Ⓐ Ⓑ Ⓒ Ⓓ
16 Ⓐ Ⓑ Ⓒ Ⓓ	36 Ⓐ Ⓑ Ⓒ Ⓓ	56 Ⓐ Ⓑ Ⓒ Ⓓ	76 Ⓐ Ⓑ Ⓒ Ⓓ
17 Ⓐ Ⓑ Ⓒ Ⓓ	37 Ⓐ Ⓑ Ⓒ Ⓓ	57 Ⓐ Ⓑ Ⓒ Ⓓ	77 Ⓐ Ⓑ Ⓒ Ⓓ
18 Ⓐ Ⓑ Ⓒ Ⓓ	38 Ⓐ Ⓑ Ⓒ Ⓓ	58 Ⓐ Ⓑ Ⓒ Ⓓ	78 Ⓐ Ⓑ Ⓒ Ⓓ
19 Ⓐ Ⓑ Ⓒ Ⓓ	39 Ⓐ Ⓑ Ⓒ Ⓓ	59 Ⓐ Ⓑ Ⓒ Ⓓ	79 Ⓐ Ⓑ Ⓒ Ⓓ
20 Ⓐ Ⓑ Ⓒ Ⓓ	40 Ⓐ Ⓑ Ⓒ Ⓓ	60 Ⓐ Ⓑ Ⓒ Ⓓ	80 Ⓐ Ⓑ Ⓒ Ⓓ

81 Ⓐ Ⓑ Ⓒ Ⓓ	101 Ⓐ Ⓑ Ⓒ Ⓓ	121 Ⓐ Ⓑ Ⓒ Ⓓ	141 Ⓐ Ⓑ Ⓒ Ⓓ
82 Ⓐ Ⓑ Ⓒ Ⓓ	102 Ⓐ Ⓑ Ⓒ Ⓓ	122 Ⓐ Ⓑ Ⓒ Ⓓ	142 Ⓐ Ⓑ Ⓒ Ⓓ
83 Ⓐ Ⓑ Ⓒ Ⓓ	103 Ⓐ Ⓑ Ⓒ Ⓓ	123 Ⓐ Ⓑ Ⓒ Ⓓ	143 Ⓐ Ⓑ Ⓒ Ⓓ
84 Ⓐ Ⓑ Ⓒ Ⓓ	104 Ⓐ Ⓑ Ⓒ Ⓓ	124 Ⓐ Ⓑ Ⓒ Ⓓ	144 Ⓐ Ⓑ Ⓒ Ⓓ
85 Ⓐ Ⓑ Ⓒ Ⓓ	105 Ⓐ Ⓑ Ⓒ Ⓓ	125 Ⓐ Ⓑ Ⓒ Ⓓ	145 Ⓐ Ⓑ Ⓒ Ⓓ
86 Ⓐ Ⓑ Ⓒ Ⓓ	106 Ⓐ Ⓑ Ⓒ Ⓓ	126 Ⓐ Ⓑ Ⓒ Ⓓ	146 Ⓐ Ⓑ Ⓒ Ⓓ
87 Ⓐ Ⓑ Ⓒ Ⓓ	107 Ⓐ Ⓑ Ⓒ Ⓓ	127 Ⓐ Ⓑ Ⓒ Ⓓ	147 Ⓐ Ⓑ Ⓒ Ⓓ
88 Ⓐ Ⓑ Ⓒ Ⓓ	108 Ⓐ Ⓑ Ⓒ Ⓓ	128 Ⓐ Ⓑ Ⓒ Ⓓ	148 Ⓐ Ⓑ Ⓒ Ⓓ
89 Ⓐ Ⓑ Ⓒ Ⓓ	109 Ⓐ Ⓑ Ⓒ Ⓓ	129 Ⓐ Ⓑ Ⓒ Ⓓ	149 Ⓐ Ⓑ Ⓒ Ⓓ
90 Ⓐ Ⓑ Ⓒ Ⓓ	110 Ⓐ Ⓑ Ⓒ Ⓓ	130 Ⓐ Ⓑ Ⓒ Ⓓ	150 Ⓐ Ⓑ Ⓒ Ⓓ
91 Ⓐ Ⓑ Ⓒ Ⓓ	111 Ⓐ Ⓑ Ⓒ Ⓓ	131 Ⓐ Ⓑ Ⓒ Ⓓ	
92 Ⓐ Ⓑ Ⓒ Ⓓ	112 Ⓐ Ⓑ Ⓒ Ⓓ	132 Ⓐ Ⓑ Ⓒ Ⓓ	
93 Ⓐ Ⓑ Ⓒ Ⓓ	113 Ⓐ Ⓑ Ⓒ Ⓓ	133 Ⓐ Ⓑ Ⓒ Ⓓ	
94 Ⓐ Ⓑ Ⓒ Ⓓ	114 Ⓐ Ⓑ Ⓒ Ⓓ	134 Ⓐ Ⓑ Ⓒ Ⓓ	
95 Ⓐ Ⓑ Ⓒ Ⓓ	115 Ⓐ Ⓑ Ⓒ Ⓓ	135 Ⓐ Ⓑ Ⓒ Ⓓ	
96 Ⓐ Ⓑ Ⓒ Ⓓ	116 Ⓐ Ⓑ Ⓒ Ⓓ	136 Ⓐ Ⓑ Ⓒ Ⓓ	
97 Ⓐ Ⓑ Ⓒ Ⓓ	117 Ⓐ Ⓑ Ⓒ Ⓓ	137 Ⓐ Ⓑ Ⓒ Ⓓ	
98 Ⓐ Ⓑ Ⓒ Ⓓ	118 Ⓐ Ⓑ Ⓒ Ⓓ	138 Ⓐ Ⓑ Ⓒ Ⓓ	
99 Ⓐ Ⓑ Ⓒ Ⓓ	119 Ⓐ Ⓑ Ⓒ Ⓓ	139 Ⓐ Ⓑ Ⓒ Ⓓ	
100 Ⓐ Ⓑ Ⓒ Ⓓ	120 Ⓐ Ⓑ Ⓒ Ⓓ	140 Ⓐ Ⓑ Ⓒ Ⓓ	

Practice Test 5

Directions: For each of the following questions, select the choice that best answers the question.

1. In joint tenancy, the right of possession indicates that each owner

   A. has the right to use all of the property.
   B. has an equal share of the property.
   C. took title with the same deed.
   D. took title at the same time.

2. Community property

   A. may be sold with the signature of either party.
   B. may be sold with the signature of either party if the property was acquired before the marriage.
   C. may be sold with the signature of one party if that party previously owned it as other than community property.
   D. must always have the signatures of both parties in order to be sold.

3. Trustor is to trustee as

   A. trustee is to grantee.
   B. trustor is to beneficiary.
   C. grantee is to grantor.
   D. grantor is to grantee.

4. Which form of business structure does not avoid double taxation?

   A. corporation
   B. S corporation
   C. limited liability corporation
   D. partnership

5. In a community property situation, which of the following is not separate property?

   A. property inherited by one spouse
   B. property purchased with the funds obtained from separate property
   C. property the parties agree to as separate
   D. property acquired with commingled funds

6. How many acres are contained in the standard section directly north of section number 16?

   A. 640 acres
   B. 320 acres
   C. 160 acres
   D. Not enough information is provided.

GO ON TO THE NEXT PAGE

155

7. Which of the following best defines a fixture?

    A. items attached to the land

    B. personal property that is permanently attached to the structure

    C. personal property that has become real property

    D. all of the above

8. The right of the municipality to install a water line underground across Owner A's property would involve the acquisition of

    A. surface rights.

    B. subsurface rights.

    C. mineral rights.

    D. air rights.

9. The state may divert water from one area to another by its

    A. littoral rights.

    B. right of appropriation.

    C. riparian rights.

    D. underground water rights.

10. Which of the following fixtures would a person correctly assume he can take with him when he moves?

    A. attached display cases used in a jewelry business in leased space

    B. chattels

    C. a built-in microwave oven in a condominium

    D. an air-conditioner built into the wall

11. An owner takes title to a property on the condition that he never use it to manufacture alcoholic beverages on the property. What term best describes his ownership interest?

    A. fee simple absolute

    B. fee simple qualified

    C. fee simple at sufferance

    D. fee simple at will

12. Owner A gives a life estate to a house he owns to his sister for the life of their mother. Upon the mother's death, possession of the house will return to the owner, unless he has died, in which case possession will go to his children, to whom he is leaving the house in his will. Identify the interests in this situation.

    A. Owner A has a remainder interest.

    B. Owner A's children have a reversionary interest.

    C. Owner A has a reversionary interest and his children have a remainder interest.

    D. Owner A's children have a life estate interest.

13. In California, if the ownership status of the property of a married couple is unclear, which of the following best describes what the courts will presume?

    A. All real property acquired during the marriage is community property.

    B. All real property in California acquired during the marriage is community property.

    C. All personal property is community property.

    D. All real property in California and all personal property anywhere is community property.

14. The terms *meridians* and *baselines* are most closely related to which system of property description?

    A. government survey

    B. metes and bounds

    C. plat map

    D. subdivision map

15. Which of the following is a general lien?

    A. property tax lien

    B. mechanic's lien

    C. mortgage

    D. judgment

16. In cases where a notice of completion or cessation was not filed by the owner, how long does someone have to file a mechanic's lien?

    A. 120 days from completion of the work

    B. 90 days from completion of the work

    C. 120 days from commencement of the work

    D. 90 days from commencement of the work

17. When a mechanic's lien has been filed and then terminated by the claimant's voluntary release, what should be filed so that no cloud appears on the title?

    A. foreclosure documents

    B. lien release

    C. notice of nonresponsibility

    D. preliminary notice of lien termination

18. An easement in gross

    A. benefits the servient tenement.

    B. benefits the dominant tenement.

    C. can only be created by eminent domain.

    D. does not run with the land.

Practice Test 5

GO ON TO THE NEXT PAGE

19. In order for a married couple to qualify for a $75,000 homestead exemption, which of the following must be true?

    A. Their homestead must be owned as community property.

    B. They must reside together.

    C. Their income must not exceed $75,000 per year.

    D. They must reinvest the money from the sale of the property within a year.

20. Owner A has an easement across Owner B's property. Owner A acquires Owner B's property. What happens to the easement?

    A. Nothing—it continues to exist.

    B. It is terminated by abandonment.

    C. It is terminated by merger.

    D. It is terminated by estoppel.

21. CC & Rs are generally enforced by

    A. the zoning enforcement office.

    B. a court injunction.

    C. a notice of foreclosure.

    D. a lien against the property.

22. An easement by prescription may be acquired after continuous, open, and notorious use for at least

    A. two years.

    B. three years.

    C. five years.

    D. ten years.

23. The zoning on a commercial lot permits coverage of 20% of the lot with a structure no greater than five stories. What is the maximum square footage that can be built on a 350×250-foot lot.

    A. 87,500

    B. 17,500

    C. 6,000

    D. 1,200

24. What do planned development, condominium, time-share, and stock cooperative projects have in common?

    A. They are all common interest subdivisions.

    B. They are all undivided interest subdivisions.

    C. They are all exempt from the Subdivided Lands Law.

    D. They are all exempt from the Subdivision Map Act.

25. Owner A needs an easement from Owner B to get to the nearby highway. Owner B agrees. Which of the following is true?

    A. Owner A reserves the easement.

    B. Owner B reserves the easement.

    C. Owner A grants the easement.

    D. Owner B grants the easement.

26. In general, which lien will have first priority of payment?

    A. property tax lien

    B. voluntary lien by date

    C. involuntary lien by date

    D. first mortgage lien

27. In a township, which section is located immediately southwest of section 22?

    A. 15

    B. 23

    C. 27

    D. 28

28. A broker who has a listing agreement to sell a house produces a buyer whose offer is acceptable to the seller. However, the seller delays title closing until after the listing agreement has expired, at which time he sells his house to the buyer. The seller then refuses to compensate the broker because the broker did not sell the house within the time frame of the listing agreement. Which of the following statements is true?

    A. The broker is entitled to his commission.

    B. The broker is entitled to a reduced commission because he exceeded the listing agreement time frame.

    C. The broker is not entitled to his commission.

    D. The matter will have to be arbitrated by the California Real Estate Commission.

29. A listing agreement between Broker A and Seller B fails to mention a specific commission amount. Most owners in the neighborhood pay their real estate brokers a 5% commission on the sale price of the property. What commission, if any, will be owed by Seller A to Broker B when the house sells?

    A. none

    B. 5%

    C. the amount arbitrated by the local real estate association

    D. 2.5%

Practice Test 5

GO ON TO THE NEXT PAGE

30. Another term for producing a ready, willing, and able buyer is a(n)

A. consummated offer.

B. arm's-length transaction.

C. meeting of the minds.

D. agreement in principle.

31. Which of the following is most correct regarding termination of a listing by a principal?

A. The principal may not terminate the listing before the expiration date.

B. The principal may terminate the listing in order to avoid paying a commission by negotiating directly with a prospective buyer produced by the broker.

C. The principal may terminate the listing with no obligation to the broker.

D. The principal may terminate the listing but may be liable for the broker's expenses up to that point.

32. A broker regularly pays a finder's fee to his barber who often sends customers to him. Which of the following is true?

A. The broker may pay such fees to anyone who solicits business for him.

B. The broker may pay this fee since the barber is also a licensed professional.

C. Payment of this fee is illegal.

D. Only the salesperson can pay this type of finder's fee to a nonlicensed person.

33. For purposes of the California Real Estate Law a salesperson is considered

A. an employee.

B. an independent contractor.

C. either an employee or an independent contractor.

D. the same as a broker.

34. When the actions of a buyer and seller seem to indicate that the seller will pay a broker a commission for selling her house but no agreement has been discussed or signed, the best description for the type of agreement, if any, that they have is a(n)

A. actual agreement.

B. implied agreement.

C. expressed agreement.

D. inherent agreement.

35. The time frame for disclosure of agency relationships is

A. at the convenience of the broker and the principal.

B. any time after signing the contract.

C. before closing.

D. as soon as it is practicable.

36. A subagent to the principal is authorized by

    A. the agent of the seller.

    B. the cooperating broker.

    C. the principal.

    D. implication.

37. A buyer's agent can receive compensation

    A. only from the buyer.

    B. from the seller or the buyer.

    C. from the seller or the buyer only if he becomes a dual agent.

    D. only from the principal.

38. An option listing agreement whereby the broker purchases the property from the seller, and then resells the property making a profit on the resale requires

    A. no special information beyond the principal signing the listing agreement.

    B. informing the principal of the resale of the property.

    C. informing the principal of the resale of the property, any profits to be realized and securing the permission of the seller to proceed.

    D. sharing the profit with the principal.

39. Which of the following is a principal not liable for?

    A. lying to the buyer about the condition of the house

    B. her broker lying about the condition of the house

    C. her subagent broker violating fair housing statutes

    D. an independent contractor sales agent assaulting a prospective buyer

40. If a buyer were to sue a broker for not properly inspecting a house and revealing material facts, she would cite which case?

    A. *United States v. Foley*

    B. *Jones v. Mayer*

    C. Treaty of Guadalupe

    D. *Easton v. Strassburger*

41. Seller A wants to use the services of a real estate professional to help her sell her house. However, she is also going to try to sell her house herself and does not want to pay a broker if she succeeds. What type of agreements should she have in order to accomplish this?

    A. open listing and net listing

    B. open listing and exclusive agency listing

    C. open listing and option listing

    D. exclusive agency listing and exclusive authorization and right-to-sell listing

GO ON TO THE NEXT PAGE

Practice Test 5

42. All agency agreements must be in writing or confirmed in writing in order to collect a commission except

    A. agency by ratification.

    B. agency by estoppel.

    C. implied agency.

    D. None of the above—there are no exceptions.

43. Which type of listing agreement would be considered a unilateral agreement?

    A. open listing

    B. net listing

    C. exclusive agency listing

    D. exclusive authorization and right-to-sell listing

44. In addition to having an independent contractor agreement, the most distinguishing factor that differentiates an independent contractor from an employee is

    A. the number of hours worked per week.

    B. the amount of compensation.

    C. the emphasis on results rather than method.

    D. whether the person is a salesperson or a broker working for another broker.

45. A seller has given an open listing to several brokers with no time limit. Broker A brings a prospective buyer to the house. A few weeks later, the owner contacts the same prospective buyer directly and negotiates a sale of the property. Which of the following statements is true?

    A. The seller owes no commission to the broker.

    B. The seller owes a reduced commission to the broker.

    C. The broker will have to collect his commission from the buyer.

    D. The seller owes the broker the commission.

46. The sale price of a four-unit residential property was $450,000. Each unit rents for $900 per month. Using the gross rent multiplier approach and the information provided, what would be the value of a similar building where each of the four units rents for $750 per month?

    A. $475,000

    B. $425,000

    C. $375,000

    D. $350,000

47. A property located near a sewage treatment plant would likely suffer from

    A. functional obsolescence curable.

    B. physical deterioration incurable.

    C. external obsolescence curable.

    D. external obsolescence incurable.

48. A building has a replacement cost of $150,000 and an estimated economic life of 50 years. What is the annual amount of depreciation?

A. $3,000
B. $4,500
C. $5,000
D. $6,000

49. A homeowner improves her house by adding a new fireplace each year for three years. She finds that the first fireplace has increased the value of her house by 150% of the cost of the fireplace. The second fireplace increased the value of the house by 100% of the cost. The third fireplace has had no effect on the value of the house. This is likely based on the principle of

A. highest and best use.
B. supply and demand.
C. progression and regression.
D. increasing and diminishing returns.

50. In calculating net operating income, when is debt service deducted from potential gross income?

A. as part of the vacancy and collection loss
B. as part of the operating expenses
C. after operating expenses are deducted
D. never

51. Fee appraisers work for

A. government agencies on federally related transactions.
B. banks and mortgage companies.
C. themselves and are hired on a project-by-project basis.
D. tax assessment offices.

52. An investment property has a net operating income of $47,700 per year. Buildings of this type are selling at a rate of return of 9%. What is the estimated value of the building?

A. $530,000
B. $524,175
C. $470,700
D. $429,300

53. Accrued depreciation is the dollar amount of

A. physical deterioration.
B. functional obsolescence.
C. external obsolescence.
D. all of the above

GO ON TO THE NEXT PAGE

Practice Test 5

54. Economic rent is the same as

    A. scheduled rent.

    B. market rent.

    C. effective gross income.

    D. net operating income.

55. A homeowner is deciding whether to do a major improvement to her home. The primary consideration is whether her home will increase in value to cover the cost of the improvement. Her concerns are based on her knowledge of the principle of

    A. contribution.

    B. change.

    C. anticipation.

    D. competition.

56. The most comprehensive type of appraisal report is

    A. the Uniform Residential Appraisal Report form.

    B. a narrative report.

    C. a letter opinion of value.

    D. an oral report.

57. In the income approach, what is the relationship between the capitalization rate and value?

    A. rate goes down, value goes down

    B. rate goes up, value stays the same

    C. rate goes down, value goes up

    D. rate goes up, value goes up

58. In appraising a 300-unit residential rental complex, an appraiser would rely most heavily on which valuation approach?

    A. income capitalization

    B. gross rent multiplier

    C. sales comparison

    D. cost

59. The reproduction cost of a building is $280,000. Accrued depreciation is estimated at $60,000. The estimated land value is $70,000. What is the estimated value of the property?

    A. $410,000

    B. $340,000

    C. $290,000

    D. $220,000

60. A house in need of painting may be said to be suffering from

    A. external obsolescence incurable.
    B. functional obsolescence curable.
    C. physical deterioration incurable.
    D. physical deterioration curable.

61. A comparable property sold three months ago for $280,000. Prices in the area have increased 5% in the past six months. What is the indicated value of a similar property?

    A. $294,000
    B. $287,000
    C. $273,000
    D. $266,000

62. The subject property is located in a neighborhood that is deemed to be inferior to the comparable. What type of adjustment is necessary in the sales comparison approach?

    A. positive to the subject
    B. negative to the subject
    C. positive to the comparable
    D. negative to the comparable

63. A high-risk investment property in a run-down neighborhood would tend to have

    A. the same capitalization rate as a low-risk investment.
    B. a higher capitalization rate than a lower-risk investment.
    C. a lower capitalization rate than a lower-risk investment.
    D. None of the above—there is no relationship between risk and the capitalization rate.

64. The FHA lends money to purchase

    A. one-family homes.
    B. agricultural properties.
    C. commercial properties.
    D. none of the above

65. A borrower obtains a fully amortized mortgage loan for $165,000 at an interest rate of 6.5% for 30 years. The monthly payments are $1,044.45. What is the balance of the principal after the first month's payment?

    A. $164,449.30
    B. $163,955.55
    C. $107,250
    D. $893.75

GO ON TO THE NEXT PAGE

Practice Test 5

66. A lender charges a loan origination fee of one point to make a mortgage loan. Most likely this point will have what effect on the nominal interest rate relative to the APR?

   A. The nominal rate will be higher than the APR.
   B. The nominal rate will be the same as the APR.
   C. The nominal rate will be lower than the APR.
   D. none of the above

67. PMI will no longer be necessary on a 100% LTV ratio loan of $178,000 when the LTV reaches 75%. The property, having appreciated in value, is now worth $210,000. How much of the principal of the loan will have to be paid off before the PMI can be dropped?

   A. None—PMI can be dropped immediately.
   B. $10,000
   C. $17,000
   D. $20,500

68. A mortgage banker pays a fee of $200 to several brokers and salespeople for each loan that she successfully closes simply for referring business to her. This is an example of a

   A. kickback and is illegal.
   B. kickback and is legal.
   C. referral fee and is legal.
   D. referral fee and is legal, as long as it does not exceed $300.

69. An impound account can be required to approve a loan if the LTV is

   A. 70%.
   B. 75%.
   C. 80%.
   D. 90%.

70. A situation where the balance of the mortgage loan actually increases while payments are being made is called

   A. reverse annuity.
   B. negative amortization.
   C. shared appreciation.
   D. growing equity.

71. Which of the following terms does not fit with the group referring to a type of mortgage payment plan?

   A. nonamortized
   B. interest only
   C. nonconforming
   D. straight note

72. The Real Estate Loan Law permits real estate brokers to do all but which of the following?

    A. lend their own money

    B. solicit loans

    C. charge negotiable commission rates on all loans

    D. negotiate loan terms

73. Which of the following is true about FHA loans?

    A. They require a prepayment penalty.

    B. They do not require mortgage insurance.

    C. They have no set interest rate.

    D. They require a down payment.

74. The VA loan program will guarantee loans for

    A. no more than the CRV.

    B. up to 10% more than the CRV.

    C. a "reasonable" amount negotiated by the buyer above the CRV.

    D. no more than 98.5% of the CRV.

75. Payment of three points on a note whose rate is 6% will increase the yield to the lender to

    A. $6\frac{1}{8}\%$

    B. $6\frac{1}{4}\%$

    C. $6\frac{3}{8}\%$

    D. $6\frac{1}{2}\%$

76. Creative financing generally does not include

    A. seller financing.

    B. installment sales.

    C. wraparound mortgages.

    D. FHA 203(b) loans.

77. Which of the following does not buy mortgages?

    A. the secondary market

    B. GNMA

    C. FNMA

    D. FHLMC

GO ON TO THE NEXT PAGE

78. In seller financing of a home purchase, which of the following is correct?

   A. The seller is the mortgagor; the buyer is the mortgagee.

   B. The seller is the trustee; the buyer is the beneficiary.

   C. The seller is the trustor; the buyer is the trustee.

   D. The seller is the mortgagee; the buyer is the mortgagor.

79. What is the first month's interest on a fixed rate loan at 7% for 25 years for a home that cost $360,000 with an LTV ratio of 80%?

   A. $1,680

   B. $2,100

   C. $20,160

   D. $25,200

80. A builder contracts with a buyer to build a home. The builder agrees to use his own funds to build the house. The builder wants a guarantee that the buyer will be able to buy the house when it is completed. What will the buyer seek from a mortgage lender?

   A. a construction loan

   B. a standby commitment

   C. an interim loan

   D. a package mortgage

81. How much total interest will a borrower pay on a $250,000, 30-year, fixed-rate, amortized loan at 5%, when the monthly payment is $1,342.50?

   A. $12,500

   B. $233,300

   C. $312,600

   D. $375,000

82. When a buyer takes over a seller's mortgage, what can the seller do to protect himself from future liability for the mortgage?

   A. He will be liable until the debt is paid off and can do nothing.

   B. He can make sure that the buyer assumes the mortgage.

   C. He can see to it that the buyer buys the house subject to the mortgage.

   D. He can get a guarantee of payment from the buyer.

83. A lender can usually invoke an acceleration clause

   A. if the borrower misses a certain number of payments.

   B. if the buyer tears down the house.

   C. if the buyer fails to pay property taxes.

   D. all of the above

84. A testator who leaves real property to his heirs is also known as a(n)

A. legatee.

B. devise.

C. administrator.

D. devisor.

85. The high-water mark in the river next to Owner A's property has permanently receded. Owner A has likely gained land area by the process of

A. reliction.

B. avulsion.

C. accretion.

D. erosion.

86. During the statutory period required to claim ownership by adverse possession, which of the following is true?

A. The claimant's occupancy of the property must be unknown to anyone.

B. The claimant pays the taxes.

C. The claimant must have the owner's permission to occupy the land.

D. The claimant must have occupied the property for a total of five years out of seven, the time period not necessarily being continuous.

87. Which of the following is not required for a deed to be recorded?

A. grantee's signature

B. acknowledgment

C. the deed in writing

D. description of the property

88. A trustee's deed is given

A. to the trustor after the debt has been paid.

B. by the trustee to the purchaser of a property after a foreclosure sale.

C. to the trustee by the beneficiary after the debt has been paid.

D. by the trustor to the trustee as security for a debt.

89. What type of relationship does an escrow agent have to the principals?

A. special agency

B. universal agency

C. limited agency

D. general agency

GO ON TO THE NEXT PAGE

169

90. Buyer A and Seller B agree to a change in the house sale transaction, which is now in escrow. Seller A informs the escrow agent of the change by phone. Which of the following is true?

A. The change will not be effective unless it is put in writing by both parties.

B. The change will not be effective under any circumstances since the original instructions take precedence.

C. The escrow agent will most likely follow the new orders, verifying it later by phone with the seller.

D. The escrow agent will make the change based on the phone call.

91. In escrow, prepaid taxes, assessments, or insurance will be a

A. credit to the buyer and a debit to the seller.

B. credit to the buyer and the seller.

C. debit to the buyer and the seller.

D. credit to the seller and a debit to the buyer.

92. The normal time frame used to calculate prorations is a

A. 365-day year.

B. 12-month year with the exact number of days each month.

C. 360-day year with the exact number of days each month.

D. 12-month year with months of 30 days each.

93. Property title insurance

A. insures the lender.

B. insures the buyer.

C. covers unknown risks to the title such as unrecorded liens.

D. all of the above

94. In an all-cash property sale, title insurance is

A. mandatory.

B. advisable.

C. unnecessary.

D. unnecessary if the title company is used as the escrow agent.

95. The base value of a property and the assessed value will be the same if

A. the property has not been sold since 1975.

B. the property has been sold since 1975.

C. the property has had no physical changes made since 1975.

D. the improvement was built this year.

96. What is the first tax installment on a property whose assessed value is $180,000, assuming the property is eligible for a homeowner's exemption?

    A. $173

    B. $865

    C. $1,730

    D. $8,650

97. Commingling is

    A. the legal mixing of the broker's money and the client's funds.

    B. the illegal mingling of the broker's money and the client's funds.

    C. the status of funds during the escrow process.

    D. the holding of funds pending acceptance of an offer.

98. How long may a deposit generally be held before an offer is accepted before it must be deposited in the broker's trust fund?

    A. indefinitely

    B. one day

    C. three days

    D. five days

99. Which of the following is not an exemption under the federal fair housing laws?

    A. sale of properties by religious organizations to its members

    B. renting of rooms in private clubs to its membership

    C. housing where all the units are all for residents 62 and older

    D. sale of an owner-occupied, single-family house based on race

100. If a local city passes a law prohibiting discrimination on the basis of sexual orientation, it is

    A. valid because it is stricter than the federal law.

    B. invalid because the federal law does not contain sexual orientation as a protected class.

    C. valid only if the state included this as a protected class.

    D. invalid unless the surrounding county also adopts the same law.

101. A real estate broker advertised a mobile home for sale that was located on a privately owned piece of property that has six months remaining on a one-year lease. Which of the following is correct?

    A. The new owner will take over the six-month lease.

    B. The broker should advertise that there is only six months left on the lease.

    C. The broker should not advertise the mobile home for sale at all.

    D. The broker can place the ad as is.

GO ON TO THE NEXT PAGE

102. An ad that does not state the name of the brokerage representing the seller is called

    A. a blind ad and is illegal.

    B. a blind ad and is legal.

    C. false advertising and is illegal.

    D. misleading advertising and is legal.

103. Assuming a transaction closes, what is the earliest date a broker can discard the records of that transaction?

    A. three years from the closing date

    B. three years from the listing date

    C. five years from the listing date

    D. seven years from the closing date

104. An employment agreement between a salesperson and a broker would cover

    A. compensation.

    B. supervision.

    C. duties.

    D. all of the above

105. An unlicensed assistant is permitted to assist a salesperson or a broker with

    A. clerical functions.

    B. management and supervisory functions.

    C. legal functions.

    D. sales functions.

106. The Department of Real Estate administers all of the following except

    A. Real Estate License Law.

    B. the Real Estate Education and Research Fund.

    C. the Real Estate Recovery Fund.

    D. the California Building Code.

107. The penalty for a Real Estate License Law violation can include

    A. a fine.

    B. suspension or revocation of the license.

    C. requiring the licensee to complete educational courses.

    D. all of the above

108. Which of the following could result in license suspension or revocation?

    A. misusing a trade name
    B. a broker not supervising her salespersons
    C. violating the restrictions of a limited license
    D. all of the above

109. How many hours of continuing education must a salesperson renewing her license for the first time complete?

    A. 5 hours
    B. 12 hours
    C. 25 hours
    D. 45 hours

110. What is the experience requirement for a non-college-educated real estate broker applicant?

    A. none
    B. one year
    C. two years
    D. five years

111. What is the maximum amount per licensee that can be paid by the Real Estate Recovery Account?

    A. $20,000
    B. $50,000
    C. $75,000
    D. $100,000

112. Realtor A suggests to a new home purchaser that the purchaser buy his appliances from the ABC appliance corporation in which the Realtor is a part owner. Which of the following is most correct with respect to the Realtor code of ethics?

    A. The Realtor has done nothing wrong.
    B. The Realtor has done nothing wrong as long as he revealed his ownership interest in the appliance store.
    C. The Realtor should have refrained from recommending his own appliance store to the purchaser.
    D. The Realtor should deduct any profit he makes on the appliances from his commission on the house sale.

113. With respect to accepting compensation from more than one party in a transaction, a Realtor

    A. may never do so.
    B. may always do so.
    C. may do so with informed consent of his client.
    D. may do so by disclosing it to all parties and obtaining informed consent of his client.

GO ON TO THE NEXT PAGE

114. A broker who wants to use a fictitious business name must do all of the following except

    A. register the name with the county clerk.

    B. check the name with the California Real Estate Commission.

    C. check the name with the county Board of Realtors.

    D. publish the name in the newspaper.

115. A real estate broker selling several mobile homes on his property

    A. may do so with his broker's license.

    B. must obtain a mobile home dealer license.

    C. can obtain a temporary mobile home license from the Department of Real Estate.

    D. needs nothing but the broker's license if the mobile homes are registered.

116. An owner of a property purchases it for $150,000 and is able to sell it for $250,000 within three months. Which of the following is correct?

    A. He must disclose his purchase price to the buyer.

    B. He must disclose his profit to the seller from whom he bought the property.

    C. If he had waited until after six months to sell the property, he would have avoided secret profit disclosure requirements.

    D. He may keep all information on the transaction confidential from all parties.

117. If a broker acts on behalf of a principal without authorization and later the principal accepts what the agent has done on his behalf, it is called a(n)

    A. agency by ratification.

    B. implied agency.

    C. unilateral agency.

    D. express agency.

118. Upon the sale of a residential rental property, the security deposit may be

    A. kept by the seller.

    B. transferred to the new owner.

    C. returned to the tenant.

    D. either B or C

119. Mello-Roos assessments

    A. must be disclosed to a prospective purchaser.

    B. need not be disclosed to a prospective purchaser.

    C. appear on the regular property tax bill.

    D. do not create a lien on the property.

120. The required physical inspection of a condominium by a real estate agent

- **A.** does not exist because it is a condominium.
- **B.** includes the unit and the common areas and nearby off-site areas.
- **C.** includes the unit and the common areas.
- **D.** includes only the unit.

121. Seller A added a new bathroom onto the house five years ago. What are his obligations to a purchaser of the house?

- **A.** He must disclose the addition and whether or not it was properly permitted.
- **B.** He must disclose the addition only if it was not properly permitted.
- **C.** He must disclose the addition to the broker and the broker must determine if it is discloseable to the buyer.
- **D.** The seller is under no obligation to disclose the addition.

122. The obligation to inspect the property for material defects belongs to

- **A.** the buyer's broker.
- **B.** the cooperating broker.
- **C.** the seller's broker.
- **D.** all of the above

123. Payments from the Real Estate Recovery Account

- **A.** are charged against the licensee involved.
- **B.** are initially funded by license fees.
- **C.** are used to compensate real estate fraud victims.
- **D.** all of the above

124. When did the Agency Relationship Disclosure Law become effective?

- **A.** 1986
- **B.** 1988
- **C.** 1990
- **D.** 1991

125. In general, when a broker is involved in arranging mortgage loans, the records must be kept for a minimum of

- **A.** two years.
- **B.** three years.
- **C.** four years.
- **D.** five years.

GO ON TO THE NEXT PAGE

126. Which of the following buyer's questions may a salesperson answer?

    A. What is the racial balance in the neighborhood?

    B. Are there a lot of children in the area?

    C. Are there a lot of married couples in the neighborhood?

    D. What is the average income of the residents of this community?

127. The maximum fine for an unlicensed person who practices real estate is

    A. $10,000

    B. $5,000

    C. $2,000

    D. $1,000

128. The seller of a commercial building with masonry construction and wood-frame floors built before what date would have to provide the buyer with a booklet entitled "Commercial Property Owner's Guide to Earthquake Safety"?

    A. January 1, 1960

    B. December 31, 1960

    C. January 1, 1975

    D. December 31, 1975

129. If the buyer of a property in an earthquake fault zone receives a copy of the "Homeowner's Guide to Earthquake Safety," the broker

    A. need not provide any additional information about earthquakes.

    B. must still disclose the fact that the property is in the earthquake zone.

    C. neither A nor B

    D. both A and B

130. If a real estate agent is employed in the sale of a house that requires a lead-based paint disclosure, the agent should do all but which of the following?

    A. advise the seller of the disclosure requirements

    B. make sure the buyer has received the lead-paint hazard booklet

    C. complete the disclosure form

    D. obtain a signed statement from the buyer indicating that she has received the proper information

131. Violations of the lead-based paint hazard disclosure requirements by a broker can result in

    A. criminal penalties.

    B. civil penalties.

    C. action under the real estate license law.

    D. all of the above

132. An agent has completed an inspection of a property she is selling and notes asbestos in the basement. She provides the buyer with the booklet entitled "Environmental Hazards: A Guide for Homeowners, Buyers, Landlords, and Tenants" and never mentions the asbestos specifically. Which of the following is true?

A. She has violated no law because she gave the buyer the booklet.

B. She must specifically disclose the presence of asbestos to the buyer.

C. She can satisfy the disclosure requirement by making sure that asbestos is noted on the seller's portion of the transfer disclosure form.

D. She can satisfy the disclosure requirement by checking to see if the asbestos appears on the inspection report done by the buyer's home inspector.

133. Owner A agrees to sell her property to Buyer B for $500,000 any time within the next year if Buyer B wishes to proceed with the sale. This is an example of a(n)

A. unenforceable contract.

B. option to purchase contract.

C. voidable contract.

D. bilateral contract.

134. Which of the following is not one of the requirements for a valid real estate sales contract?

A. It must be in writing.

B. It must have a consideration.

C. It must be witnessed.

D. It must be an offer and acceptance.

135. Buyer A loses his job after he has signed an agreement to buy a piece of property. Because he can longer afford to buy the property by himself, he finds someone who will share the purchase price. The seller agrees to sell the property to the two buyers. What would the substitute contract be called?

A. a novation

B. a release

C. a discharge

D. an assignment

136. Broker A agrees to represent Seller B, who wants to sell her home. Seller B agrees to pay Broker A if he can sell the house, but they are old friends and have no written agreement. The listing agreement is

A. implied, bilateral, and valid.

B. implied, bilateral, and void.

C. expressed, bilateral, and void.

D. expressed, unilateral, and void.

GO ON TO THE NEXT PAGE

137. A buyer's agency agreement generally advises the buyer

    A. that the broker may collect a fee from the seller.

    B. that the broker may also represent the seller.

    C. that all commissions are negotiable.

    D. all of the above

138. An offer once made but before it is accepted

    A. can be revoked.

    B. cannot be revoked.

    C. can be revoked only if it was made orally.

    D. cannot be revoked unless the written offer included a revocation clause.

139. Buyer A offers to purchase Seller B's house for $400,000. Seller B says he will not accept anything less than $450,000. Buyer A does not respond to the counteroffer one way or the other. After a few weeks go by with no other offers, Seller B contacts Buyer A again and says he will take the $400,000 offered. Which of the following is true?

    A. Buyer A and Seller B have reached a meeting of the minds.

    B. Buyer A must stand by his offer of $400,000.

    C. Buyer A must affirm the $400,000 offer in order for there to be a valid contract.

    D. As long all the previous offers and counteroffers were made in writing, there is mutual assent at this point.

140. Personal property is generally transferred by a

    A. conveyance.

    B. deed.

    C. bill of sale.

    D. grant.

141. Who must perform in an option agreement?

    A. the buyer of the property

    B. the seller of the property

    C. the optionee

    D. the grantor

142. A listing agreement is

    A. revocable by the principal but not the agent.

    B. revocable by the agent but not the principal.

    C. revocable without penalty by either the agent or the principal.

    D. revocable with potential liability by the principal or the agent.

143. Which of the following is correct?

    A. The landlord is the lessor who has a leasehold interest.

    B. The landlord is the lessee who has the leased fee interest.

    C. The tenant is the lessor who has the leased fee interest.

    D. The tenant is the lessee who has the leasehold interest.

144. Owner A wants to rent a room in her house. Which of the following advertisements would be considered legal?

    A. Room for rent; female only

    B. Room for rent; Christian only

    C. Room for rent; Latino only

    D. all of the above

145. Which of the following is not true regarding a tenant's possessions after eviction?

    A. They belong to the landlord.

    B. They must be inventoried.

    C. They may be sold at auction.

    D. They must be stored for 30 days.

146. How many times may a mobile home owner cure a default in payment in a 12-month period?

    A. unlimited

    B. five times

    C. two times

    D. one time

147. Generally speaking, a contract entered into under duress or threat is

    A. voidable.

    B. void.

    C. unenforceable.

    D. valid.

148. The time frame in which a suit must be brought in order to enforce a contract is usually referred to as the

    A. statutory period.

    B. statute of frauds period.

    C. statute of limitations.

    D. tacking period.

Practice Test 5

GO ON TO THE NEXT PAGE

149. Which of the following answer choices does not fit with the others?

    A. mortgage and hypothecation

    B. promissory note and payment plan

    C. deed of trust and hypothecation

    D. mortgage and security instrument

150. A promise to pay off a loan to purchase a house is usually made by means of a

    A. mortgage.

    B. hypothecation.

    C. promissory note.

    D. deed of trust.

Answer Key for Practice Test 5

1. A	36. C	71. C
2. D	37. B	72. C
3. D	38. C	73. D
4. A	39. D	74. A
5. D	40. D	75. C
6. A	41. B	76. D
7. D	42. D	77. B
8. B	43. A	78. D
9. B	44. C	79. A
10. A	45. D	80. B
11. B	46. C	81. B
12. C	47. D	82. B
13. D	48. A	83. D
14. A	49. D	84. D
15. D	50. D	85. A
16. B	51. C	86. B
17. B	52. A	87. A
18. D	53. D	88. B
19. B	54. B	89. C
20. C	55. A	90. A
21. B	56. B	91. D
22. C	57. C	92. D
23. A	58. A	93. D
24. A	59. C	94. B
25. D	60. D	95. D
26. A	61. B	96. B
27. D	62. D	97. B
28. A	63. B	98. A
29. B	64. D	99. D
30. C	65. B	100. A
31. D	66. B	101. C
32. C	67. D	102. A
33. A	68. A	103. A
34. B	69. D	104. D
35. D	70. B	105. A

106. D	**121.** A	**136.** D
107. D	**122.** D	**137.** D
108. D	**123.** D	**138.** A
109. B	**124.** B	**139.** C
110. C	**125.** C	**140.** C
111. D	**126.** D	**141.** B
112. B	**127.** A	**142.** D
113. D	**128.** C	**143.** D
114. C	**129.** D	**144.** A
115. B	**130.** C	**145.** A
116. D	**131.** D	**146.** C
117. A	**132.** B	**147.** A
118. D	**133.** B	**148.** C
119. A	**134.** C	**149.** B
120. D	**135.** A	**150.** C

Answers and Explanations for Practice Test 5

1. **A.** Choice B is unity of interest, Choice C is unity of title, and Choice D is unity of time.

2. **D.** Although some of the wrong answer choices sound plausible, two signatures are always required to sell community property.

3. **D.** The trustor conveys title to the trustee. The grantor conveys title to the grantee.

4. **A.** The other three forms of organization avoid double taxation.

5. **D.** The word *commingled* means mixed, combined, or no longer separate. Such funds are considered community property.

6. **A.** This is a bit of a trick question. All standard sections in a township contain 640 acres.

7. **D.** The definition of *fixture* includes all of these forms of description.

8. **B.** Subsurface rights are related to things like the installation for pipes and other structures below the surface of the ground.

9. **B.** The state may enjoy the rights stated in the incorrect answers but diversion of water specifically falls under the state's right of appropriation.

10. **A.** These are known as trade fixtures and can normally be removed when the lease expires. *Chattel* is another word for personal property and while personal property can obviously be removed, chattels are not fixtures so the answer does not apply to the question.

11. **B.** Choices C and D are a made up combination of fee simple ownership and types of leasehold estates.

12. **C.** A life estate that comes back to the person granting it is a reversionary interest. If possession goes to a third party, in this case the owner's children, they have a remainder interest.

13. **D.** Although all the incorrect answer choices have some element of correctness, the most completely correct choice is D.

14. **A.** This is a memorization issue. Choices C and D are different names for the same system.

15. **D.** Judgments can result in liens against all property owned rather than the specific property secured for the debt.

16. **B.** This is a piece of the law you'll have to remember.

17. **B.** A foreclosure enforces the lien. Notice of nonresponsibility deals with prevention of unauthorized work. Choice D is made up.

18. **D.** Because an easement in gross does not involve an adjacent landowner, there is no dominant and servient tenement. Any easement can be created in a number of ways, including by contract. An easement in gross does not run with the land.

19. **B.** The only one of these answers that is a requirement is the definition of a married couple as a family unit that requires them to reside together.

20. **C.** When the servient and dominant tenements are joined, the easement terminates by merger.

21. **B.** These are covenant, conditions, and restrictions and are enforced usually by the neighbors through an injunction when a violation occurs.

22. **C.** Five years is the statutory period in the law.

23. **A.** First, you calculate the total area of the lot:

    350 feet × 250 feet = 87,500 square feet

    Then you calculate the area allowed to be covered (20%):

    87,500 square feet × 0.20 = 17,500 square feet

Then you multiply by the five-story height of the building:

17,500 square feet × 5 stories = 87,500 square feet

24. A. They are all common interest subdivisions and are subject to the appropriate subdivision laws.

25. D. These properties are already separate, so Owner B grants (gives or sells) the easement to Owner A.

26. A. There are some specific exceptions to this, but, in general, property tax liens take priority.

27. D. You'll probably have to draw the sections in a township to answer this question. Numbering starts in the upper-right-hand corner moving right to left, then left to right in the next row down, and alternating thereafter. You'll also have to remember your directions with the convention of north to the top, south to the bottom, east to the right, and west to the left.

6	5	4	3	2	1
7	8	9	10	11	12
18	17	16	15	14	13
19	20	21	22	23	24
30	29	28	27	26	25
31	32	33	34	35	36

28. A. The principal cannot take an action like delaying the closing and then attempt to benefit by it by claiming the listing agreement was not fulfilled.

29. B. State law indicates that in the absence of specifying a fee, the prevailing rate in the neighborhood will apply.

30. C. *Meeting of the minds* is the commonly accepted term for the point at which a commission is earned by the agent producing a ready, willing, and able buyer.

31. D. Choice D is the best answer of all the choices.

32. C. Payment of fees to any person not holding a real estate broker's license for performing real estate activities is prohibited. *Remember:* Salespeople always work for brokers.

33. A. State law considers salespersons employees for purposes of supervision by the broker.

34. B. An implied agreement exists when it can be inferred from the actions of the parties.

35. D. The language of the law is very specific here.

36. C. Subagency is established by authorization of the principal, sometimes through MLS agreements.

37. B. Fiduciary duty to the principal is not governed by who pays.

38. C. Informing is not enough—permission is also required.

39. D. The clearest answer here is Choice D, because this is a *tort* (any wrongful action except a breach of contract for which someone may be sued civilly) committed by an independent contractor.

40. D. This case established the obligation of brokers to do a reasonable inspection of the property and share this information with the buyer.

41. B. These are the two types of listings where the principal does not have to pay if she sells the property herself.

42. D. In order to enforce collection of a commission, an agency agreement must be in writing or be confirmed in writing after the fact.

43. A. *Unilateral* implies that only one party is required to act. The open listing agreement is the only one of the choices in which the broker does not agree to market the property.

44. C. Of all the choices, in addition to a written agreement, an independent contractor is hired to produce results with no direction as to how those results are to be achieved.

45. D. The seller cannot get out of paying the commission when the prospective buyer was introduced by the broker.

46. C. First, you should calculate the total gross rent of the comparison building:

4 units × $900 per unit = $3,600 gross rent

Then you need to find the gross rent multiplier:

Sales Price ÷ Gross Rent = Gross Rent Multiplier

$450,000 ÷ $3,600 = 125

Then, to get the value of the building you're interested in, you use the following formula:

Gross Rent × Gross Rent Multiplier = Value

($750 × 4 units) × 125 = $375,000

$3,000 × 125 = $375,000

47. D. Any factor that negatively affects property values and is not in or on the property itself is generally considered external obsolescence, which is always incurable.

48. A. Here's the formula:

Replacement/Reproduction Cost ÷ Economic Life = Annual Amount of Depreciation

$150,000 ÷ 50 years = $3,000

49. D. Increasing and diminishing returns relates the cost of something to the effect it has on increasing value up to the point where it no longer has a positive effect on value.

50. D. Net operating income is an analysis of the building not the investor. Debt service is attributable to the individual investor and not the building, so it is never deducted in order to arrive at net operating income.

51. C. The concept of the fee appraiser is that the appraiser works independently and, therefore, can remain objective when doing appraisals.

52. A. This problem requires the use of the formula for the income capitalization approach:

Net Operating Income ÷ Capitalization Rate = Value

$47,700 ÷ 0.09 = $530,000

53. D. Accrued depreciation is a total of depreciation from all causes.

54. B. The term *economic rent* is the same as the market rent, or what the market is currently paying for the rented space rather than what the lease requires (scheduled rent), which may be higher, lower, or the same.

55. A. The principle of contribution states that the worth of an improvement to real property is the added value it adds to the property, not its cost.

56. B. Although the form is the most common type of report for single-family homes, the narrative is the most comprehensive type of appraisal report and is commonly used for commercial buildings.

57. C. The capitalization rate is also a rate of return. If the rate of return goes down, and the income stays the same, you will spend more to buy the property (the investment).

58. A. Don't be confused by the fact that this is a residential complex. It is primarily an investment property and, as such, would be appraised using the income approach.

59. C. This question requires you to remember the cost approach formula:

Reproduction/Replacement Cost – Accrued Depreciation + Land Value = Property Value

$280,000 – $60,000 + $70,000 = $290,000

60. D. Maintenance items that return more of their value than they cost are usually classified as physical deterioration curable. Painting is generally considered to increase the value of a building by more than its cost.

61. B. Increases in value over time are added to the comparable. This problem requires you to use only three months' appreciation, which is half of the 5% appreciation over the past six months.

5% ÷ 2 = 2.5%

$280,000 × 0.025 = $7,000

$280,000 + $7,000 = $287,000

62. D. Choices A and B are wrong because you never adjust the subject. If the comparable is better, which is the case here, the adjustment to the comparable is negative.

63. B. If you analyze this question carefully, you'll see that choices A and D are essentially the same. Remember that the capitalization rate is a measure of the rate of return. Investors want a higher rate of return for high-risk investments.

64. D. This may be viewed as a trick question, since the FHA does not make purchase loans at all but rather insures loans made by primary lending institutions that are participating FHA-approved lenders.

65. B. *Remember:* The monthly payment on an amortized loan includes principal and interest.

$165,000 (Loan Amount) × 0.065 (Annual Interest Rate) = $10,725 (First Year's Interest)

$10,725 (First Year's Interest) ÷ 12 months = $893.75 (First Month's Interest Payoff)

$1,044.45 (First Month's Principal and Interest Payment) – $893.75 (First Month's Interest Payoff) = $150.70 (Principal Payoff)

$165,000 (Loan Amount) – $150.70 (First Month's Principal Payoff) = $164,849.30 balance

66. B. A discount point will change the APR relative to the nominal rate. A point used as an origination fee will usually have no effect on the APR relative to the nominal rate.

67. D. PMI can be dropped when the loan amount reaches 75% of the value of the property. If the property is now worth $210,000, then:

$210,000 × 0.75 = $157,500 (the amount to which the loan must be reduced)

$178,000 (original loan amount) – $157,500 = $20,500 (the amount that must be paid off)

68. A. Kickbacks, which in this case are payments to someone who has not provided any loan services, are illegal.

69. D. There are several conditions under which an impound account may be required, an LTV of 90% is one of them.

70. B. Amortization means paying off the loan as you go. Reverse means just the opposite (that is, adding to it).

71. C. The other three answers refer to a situation where the balance of the loan is paid off at the end.

72. C. Commission limits are set for certain loans.

73. D. FHA loans are not insured for the full value or sales price of the house. Therefore, a small down payment is required.

74. A. The buyer can pay more than the Certificate of Reasonable Value, but the program will only insure the CRV amount.

75. C. Each point increases the yield to a lender by approximately ⅛%.

76. D. Government-sponsored programs are not considered creative financing.

77. B. GNMA guarantees payments will be made to buyers of mortgages but does not actually buy mortgages.

78. D. The mortgagor (borrower) gives the mortgage (security document) to the mortgagee (lender). In this case, the seller takes back a mortgage that the buyer gives.

79. A. The term of the mortgage is irrelevant.

$360,000 (Price of House) × 0.80 (LTV) = $288,000 (Mortgage Amount)

$288,000 (Mortgage Amount) × 0.07 = $20,160 (First Year's Interest)

$20,160 (First Year's Interest) ÷ 12 months = $1,680 (First Month's Interest)

80. B. A standby commitment assures the buyer and, in turn, the builder that funds will be available at a future date.

81. B. The thing to remember here is that each payment is part principal and part interest and that everything you pay back is interest except for the amount of the original principal. Also the 5% is irrelevant to calculate the answer.

$1,342.50 (Monthly Payment of Principal and Interest) × 12 months × 30 years = $483,300 (Total Payments)

$483,300 (Total Payments for the Life of the Loan) – $250,000 (Original Principal) = $233,300 (Interest Paid)

82. B. The seller will no longer be liable if the buyer assumes the mortgage. Choices A and D are not correct, and a seller remains liable if the buyer buys the house subject to the mortgage.

83. D. All these reasons can trigger the acceleration clause where the lender can demand full payment of the loan immediately.

84. D. This is definitional.

85. A. Accretion is the gradual depositing of new soil. The other wrong answer choices involve loss of land, not increases.

86. B. The opposite is true of each of the incorrect answers.

87. A. A deed must be valid to be recorded and a valid deed does not require the grantee's signature.

88. B. Choice D is a trust deed. Choice A is a deed of reconveyance.

89. C. The escrow agent acts on behalf of each principal in turn.

90. A. The change must be made in writing and signed by both parties.

91. D. Because the seller has already paid the prepaid item, he gets a credit and the buyer owes the seller for the item so the buyer is charged with a debit (debt).

92. D. Choice C is the obvious wrong answer because it's mathematically impossible.

93. D. Title insurance covers all these things.

94. B. Title insurance is always advisable but not mandatory. However, it will be mandatory when lender financing is used.

95. D. The law says that new construction will be assessed at its new value (base rate) plus annual inflation. Because it is new this year, there would be no inflation factor, so for this year only, the base value and the assessed value would be the same.

96. B. Here's the math:

$180,000 (Assessed Value) – $7,000 (Homeowner's Exemption) = $173,000 (Taxable Value)

$173,000 (Taxable Value) × 0.01 (Tax Rate) = $1,730 (Annual Tax)

$1,730 (Annual Tax) × 0.50 = $865 (First Tax Payment)

97. B. Commingling is the mixing of broker's and client's funds and it is illegal.

98. A. Generally, the deposit is not deposited until the offer is accepted.

99. D. The 1866 Civil Rights Act prohibits discrimination on the basis of race, with no exceptions.

100. A. States and local jurisdictions can generally pass antidiscrimination laws that are more strict than the federal laws.

101. C. The law requires that the mobile home must be able to remain in place for at least a year in order for it to be advertised for sale.

102. A. This is the definition of a blind ad.

103. A. Records must be kept three years from the closing date or three years from the listing date if the transaction didn't close.

104. D. All of these items would be covered.

105. A. This is essentially what an unlicensed assistant does.

106. D. This is definitional with respect to the Department of Real Estate's authority.

107. D. Any or all of these in addition to other penalties can be imposed.

108. D. Any of these actions could result in temporary or permanent loss of the license.

109. B. The first salesperson renewal requires fewer hours than the regular (45 hours) renewal.

110. C. This is statutory.

111. D. This is statutory.

112. B. As long as he reveals his interest to the purchaser, he has not violated the code of ethics.

113. D. Both parties must be informed, and consent of the client must be obtained.

114. C. Checking with the Board of Realtors may be a good idea, but because it is not governmental, it is not legally required.

115. B. The cutoff for the additional license is two or more registered homes.

116. D. The secret profit disclosure rules apply to brokers and salespersons, not to private individuals.

117. A. This is definitional.

118. D. This is statutory.

119. A. This is the only answer that is correct.

120. D. This is statutory.

121. A. This is statutory.

122. D. This is statutory.

123. D. This is statutory.

124. B. This is statutory.

125. C. This is statutory.

126. D. Each of the other choices deals with a protected class in federal and/or California law.

127. A. This is statutory.

128. C. This is statutory.

129. D. This is statutory.

130. C. The agent should do all the things stated except complete the form for the seller.

131. D. This is statutory.

132. B. Although Choice C might practically satisfy disclosure, technically the broker must complete the inspection portion of the transfer disclosure form and note the asbestos.

133. B. The option agreement is a valid contract, and it is unilateral because only one party must act.

134. C. The contract need not be witnessed.

135. A. This is a new contract replacing the old one.

136. D. Listing agreements are unilateral and they must be in writing.

137. D. The word *advises* simply means "notifies," so buyers are notified of these possibilities.

138. A. An offer can always be revoked before acceptance by the offeree.

139. C. As soon as Seller A counteroffered with the $450,000 price, the original $400,000 offer was considered rejected and removed from consideration. The buyer would have to reaffirm this offer for a contract to exist.

140. C. This is definitional and statutory.

141. B. The seller must sell if the buyer exercises his option. The optionee is the prospective buyer because he received the option.

142. D. Either part may unilaterally revoke the agreement, but the person who revoked may be liable for expenses or other financial damages.

143. D. The landlord is the lessor and has the leased fee interest.

144. A. A gender preference advertisement in the case of a room for rent in a house that is also occupied by the owner is acceptable.

145. A. This is statutory.

146. C. This is statutory.

147. A. Although you could argue that choices B and C may be correct, technically the contract could be affirmed after the threat is removed or it could be voided at that time. So it's considered voidable.

148. C. This is definitional.

149. B. The other three choices all deal with the security instrument in mortgage loans rather than the promise to pay.

150. C. The other three choices have to do with the use of the real estate as security for the debt.

Math Review

The State of California expects its real estate salespersons and brokers to be able to do basic math as it relates to the real estate business. For the most part, this is middle-school- and high-school-level math: word problems using basic calculations (addition, subtraction, multiplication, and division) with a real estate twist. But math is math and for many people it is an intimidating subject.

If you want to brush up on your math skills, you can use this appendix, which is a review of some of the basic math you're expected to know and may be tested on. Nothing beats practice when you're trying to learn math. So after you've reviewed these sample problems, if you feel you need more work, have someone you know make up different problems based on the ones in this section.

My advice is to save all the math problems for the end of the test. You have 3 hours and 15 minutes to complete the exam, so you should have plenty of time to go back and do the math problems. Math problems take longer to compute, so why use precious time up front when you can get all the other questions done first? Although you might statistically have the potential of 8 to 12 math problems on your state exam, most people see far fewer math problems on their exam. The bottom line: You could literally skip all the math problems and still pass the exam.

That said, remember to read the math questions carefully. Make sure you do all the steps. Do them twice if you have time. And relax. Even if you find the math a little difficult, you can still do well on the exam by focusing on the other areas. After a few months as a real estate agent, you'll be able to calculate your commission down to the nearest penny in your head.

Percentages

Many real estate calculations are based on percentages. Perhaps most important of all, the calculation of a commission and its splits with other brokers and salespersons are based on percentages. Also, when two or more people own unequal shares of property, percentages may be used to calculate the value of each share. Valuation calculations may also use percentages when comparing one property to another.

Whether you use a calculator or do problems with pencil and paper, you'll always need to convert a percentage to a decimal number. There are two ways to do this:

- You can divide the percent by 100.
- You can move the decimal point two places to the left. If you choose this method, always remember that, in a whole number, the decimal is usually not shown but is implied at the end of the number.

Whichever method you use here are some examples of what you'll get:

$7\% = 0.07$
$23\% = 0.23$
$5.6\% = 0.056$
$120\% = 1.20$

One other thing to remember is that, in order to convert a fraction to a decimal, you divide the *denominator* (the bottom number in a fraction) into the *numerator* (the top number in a fraction). For example ¼ becomes $1 \div 4 = 0.25$. Basic percentage calculations are pretty straightforward.

> **Example 1:** If Owner A owns a 60% share of a building worth $500,000, how much is Owner A's share worth?
> $500,000 \times 0.60 = 300,000$

Commission problems are done the same way.

> **Example 2:** What is the commission on a $200,000 sale if the commission rate is 6%?
>
> $200,000 \times 0.06 = $12,000

A variation on the commission problem has to do with how much the owner receives after paying the commission, sometimes called *net to owner.*

> **Example 3:** Suppose you sell a property for $100,000 at a 5% commission. How much does the owner receive after the transaction?
>
> $100,000 (sale price) $\times$ 0.05 (commission rate) = $5,000 (commission)
>
> $100,000 (sale price) – $5,000 (commission) = $95,000 (net to owner)

Now suppose we ask the question in a different way.

> **Example 4:** After paying a 5% commission, the owner wants to net $95,000. What should the sale price of the property be?

The easiest thing to do is to add 5% to the $95,000, right? Wrong! Here's the proof that it's wrong:

> $95,000 (net to owner) $\times$ 0.05 (commission rate) = $4,750 (commission)
>
> $95,000 (net to owner) + $4,750 (commission) = $99,750 (sale price)

Because the owner wants $95,000 net after paying your commission, you'll have to settle for $4,750 rather than $5,000. So how do you do this calculation? Here's the formula:

> Net to Owner $\div$ (100% – Commission Rate) = Sale Price

Using the numbers in Example 4:

> $95,000 $\div$ (100% – 5%) = Sale Price
>
> $95,000 $\div$ 0.95 = $100,000

You would need to sell the house for $100,000 to have a net to owner of $95,000. Note that I changed 95% to the decimal of 0.95 by moving the decimal point two places to the left (or doing 95 $\div$ 100).

Here are some different numbers to show a variation of this method in case you run into it on the exam:

> **Example 5:** You receive a $7,000 commission, which is 4% of the selling price. What did the property sell for?

The formula in this case is:

> Commission (in dollars) $\div$ Commission Rate = Sale Price
>
> $7,000 $\div$ 0.04 = $175,000

Note: All commission rates in this section are made up for illustrative purposes only.

Area and Volume

Some basic calculations you need to know have to do with finding the area and volume of various figures. This will also require some knowledge of units of measure.

Sometimes test writers will ask for answers in different units requiring conversion. You'll want to memorize the following common conversion factors:

- **To convert inches to feet,** divide by 12 inches.
- **To convert feet to yards,** divide by 3 feet.

- **To convert feet to miles,** divide by 5,280 feet.
- **To convert square feet to acres,** divide by 43,560 square feet (ft^2).
- **To convert square feet to square yards,** divide by 9 square feet (ft^2).
- **To convert cubic feet to cubic yards,** divide by 27 cubic feet (ft^3).

Area of a square or rectangle

The basic formula for both of these calculations is

Area = Length × Width

The units must be the same (yards × yards, feet × feet, inches × inches, and so on). And the answer will always be in square units of the unit you're using.

Be cautious on the exam: Sometimes the test writers will list the right numbers but show them as yards, feet, or inches instead of *square* yards, feet, or inches.

Example 1: What is the area of a square where each side measures 40 feet?

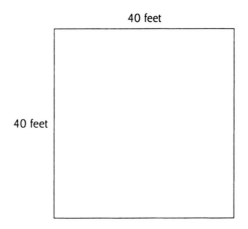

40 feet

40 feet

Area = 40 feet × 40 feet = 1,600 square feet

Example 2: What is the area of a rectangle that measures 30 feet by 50 feet?

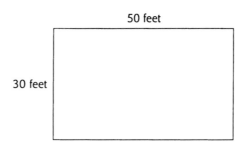

50 feet

30 feet

Area = 30 feet × 50 feet = 1,500 square feet

Area of a triangle

The basic formula for the area of a triangle is

Area = ½ × Base × Height

You may have learned this in school as

Area = (Base × Height) ÷ 2

Either formula works.

Remember when using a calculator that 0.5 is the decimal equivalent of the fraction ½.

Example 1: What is the area of a triangle whose base is 30 feet and whose height is 15 feet?

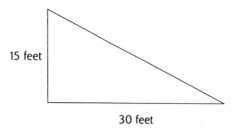

Area = 0.5 × 30 feet × 15 feet = 225 square feet

Example 2: What is the area of the following figure?

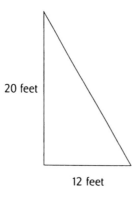

Area = 0.5 × 12 feet × 20 feet = 120 square feet

Area of an irregular shape

Many houses are not perfect squares or rectangles. The standard way to deal with calculating the area of an irregularly shaped figure is to divide it up into squares, rectangles, and triangles as necessary; then calculate the area of each of the separate figures and add them up to get the total area.

Volume of a cube or rectangular solid

When you add a third dimension to a square or a rectangle, you get a cube or a rectangular solid, respectively. Calculating the volume of a cube or rectangular solid is a matter of placing a third number, usually referred to as the *height*, into the basic area formula (see the "Area of a square or rectangle" section earlier):

Volume = Length × Width × Height

Remember: All the units of measure should be the same. The answer will be in cubic units.

Example 1: What is the volume of a room measuring 10 feet long by 10 feet wide, with 10-foot ceilings?

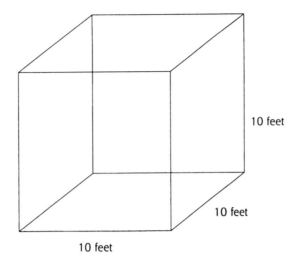

10 feet

10 feet

10 feet

In this example, the 10-foot ceilings are the height of the room, so the formula would look like this:

Volume = 10 feet × 10 feet × 10 feet = 1,000 cubic feet

Example 2: What is the volume of a room measuring 20 feet long by 15 feet wide, with 9-foot ceilings?

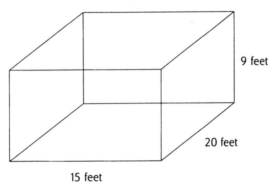

9 feet

20 feet

15 feet

Volume = 20 feet × 15 feet × 9 feet = 2,700 cubic feet

Example 3: What is the volume of a concrete slab patio that is 30 feet long by 20 feet wide by 3 inches deep?

Remember: You must convert the inches to a portion of a foot to use the formula Volume = Length × Width × Height. (See the conversion formulas earlier in this appendix for reference.)

Volume = 30 feet × 20 feet × (3 ÷ 12)
Volume = 30 feet × 20 feet × 0.25 feet = 150 cubic feet

Hint: Don't convert everything to inches. The numbers get too big to work with.

Volume of a three-dimensional triangular figure or a pyramid

In real estate, you're likely to encounter three-dimensional triangular figures or pyramids when you're dealing with roofs and attic spaces. A *front-gabled* or *side-gabled roof* is a three-dimensional triangular figure—it has a roofline, and it's the most common kind of roof. You may also find a *hipped roof,* which is shaped like a pyramid.

Here's what a three-dimensional triangular figure looks like:

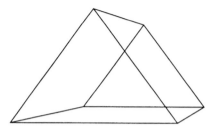

And here's the formula for the volume of this kind of figure:

Volume = Area of Triangular End × Length

Remember that the area of a triangle is ½ × Base × Height.

Example 1: Find the volume of an attic that's 20 feet wide by 25 feet long with a roof peak that's 10 feet high.

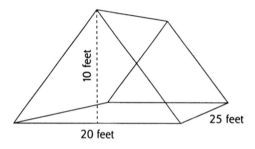

Volume = (½ × 20 feet × 10 feet) × 25 feet = 2,500 cubic feet

A pyramid looks like this:

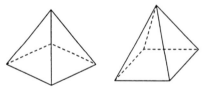

And here's the formula for the volume of a pyramid:

Volume = ⅓ × Area of the Base × Height

Remember that the area of the base is Length × Width.

Example 2: Find the volume of an attic that's 30 feet long by 25 feet wide with a peak that's 15 feet high.

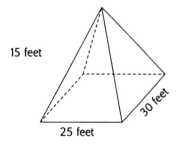

Volume = ⅓ × (25 feet × 30 feet) × 15 feet = 3,750 cubic feet

Mortgage Calculations

Several types of mortgage calculation questions appear on the exam. Here are some examples:

Example 1: What is the first year's interest on a mortgage for $200,000 at 6% interest for 30 years?

Unless otherwise stated, interest is always assumed to be annual. For this type of question, the entire balance is considered to be outstanding in the first year (or an interest-only loan). The term of the mortgage doesn't matter.

$200,000 (amount of mortgage) × 0.06 (interest rate) = $12,000 (interest due the first year)

Example 2: Using the figures in the previous example, if the loan is an amortized loan, how much interest is due the first month?

$12,000 (first year's interest) ÷ 12 months = $1,000 (interest due the first month)

Example 3: Using the information in the previous example, assuming that the monthly *payment* is $1,300, what is the balance owed on the mortgage after the first month's payment is made?

$1,300 (total payment) – $1,000 (interest) = $300 (principal paid)

$200,000 (original mortgage amount) – $300 (first month's principal payment) = $199,700 (balance)

Remember: In an amortized mortgage, each payment is made up of principal and interest.

Another common mortgage question asks you to calculate the amount necessary to *amortize* (or pay off) a certain amount of mortgage at a certain interest rate for a certain term given a monthly payment of a certain amount per $1,000 of mortgage.

Example 4: A 20-year mortgage at 5½% carries a monthly payment of $6.60 per thousand. What is the total monthly payment for a $275,000 mortgage?

$275,000 ÷ $1,000 = 275 units of $1,000 each

275 × $6.60 (payment per thousand) = $1,815 per month

Proration

Proration problems are sometimes asked on real estate exams whether or not it is common in your area to close title through an escrow agent or in a face-to-face closing. The theory of proration is quite simple, and understanding the theory helps you understand the math.

Taxes (or any other costs such as homeowners' association fees) are paid either in advance or in arrears for a certain period of time. If taxes are paid in advance, it means that the owner pays the taxes and then, in a sense, uses up those taxes as he continues to live in his home. If taxes are paid in arrears, it means the owner has used the property before he has paid the taxes for that period of use. *Proration* is simply reconciling the payment with the period of time that the property was used.

Let's look at a simple example:

Say I pay $4,800 a year in taxes and I pay them on July 1 in advance for the coming year. Now let's assume I close on the sale of the house on January 1 of that tax year. In a sense, I have only used up six months of the taxes I paid yet I paid for the whole year. At the closing, the buyer who will be living in the house for the last six months of the tax year has to pay $2,400, which are the taxes for the period he'll be living in the house. He pays me, not the city because I've already paid the taxes for the whole year.

If the taxes were normally paid in arrears, the situation would be reversed. Say the new owner paid the city $4,800 on June 30 for the previous tax year and the same closing occurred on January 1. I would be the one who would have lived in the house for free (that is, having paid no taxes for the six months I lived there). In this case, I would owe the buyer $2,400 because he would be expected to pay for the whole tax year even though he lived in the house for only six months.

If closing occurs at the end or beginning of a month, the numbers are pretty easily divided. But, of course, closings can occur on any date. Local customs and bank and title requirements may vary, but if a question does not specify, assume all months are divided into 30 days and the buyer is responsible for costs on the day of closing.

Example 1: Taxes of $1,800 are paid in advance on July 1 for the following six months. Closing occurs on October18. What is the tax proration?

$1,800 ÷ 6 months = $300 per month

$300 per month ÷ 30 days per month = $10 per day

Counting from the date of payment, the current owner owns the house for 3 months (July, August, September) and 17 days in October. (**Remember:** The buyer owns the house on the day of closing.) The buyer will own the house for the remainder of the six-month tax payment period—two months and 13 days (November, December, and 13 days in January).

2 months × $300 per month = $600

13 days × $10 per day = $130

$600 + $130 = $730

Because the seller paid the taxes in advance, the buyer owes the seller $730. In proration terminology, the seller gets a credit and the buyer gets a debit for the $730.

Note: For exam purposes, the terms *tax year* and *fiscal year* could be used interchangeably.

Appraisal and Valuation

Appraisal and valuation are extremely complex subjects, but there are some basic mathematical formulas that examiners expect you to be able to handle. In general, the formulas deal with the income approach to appraising commercial properties. The basic formulas and their variations follow.

Capitalization

Income ÷ Capitalization Rate = Value

Income ÷ Value = Capitalization Rate

Capitalization Rate × Value = Income

Income refers to *net operating income,* which is income after certain expenses have been deducted. The *capitalization rate* is often referred to as the *rate of return. Property value* is the same as the sale price when this formula is used.

Example 1: Calculate the value of a building whose net operating income is $32,000 when the capitalization rate is 8%.

$32,000 ÷ 0.08 = $400,000

Example 2: Calculate the capitalization rate of a building that sold for $720,000 with an income of $90,000.

$90,000 ÷ $720,000 = 0.125 or 12.5%

Example 3: What is the income of a building that you paid $650,000 for at a rate of return of 7%?

$650,000 × 0.07 = $45,000

Remember: All the numbers in these formulas are annual. If you're given a monthly income, you have to first multiply it by 12.

Note: When doing calculations on your calculator, you might get something like 166.66666666. On some calculators, it isn't unusual for you to see answers with several digits after the decimal point. Rounding to two places past the decimal is pretty typical. In some exams, the test writer will round the answer to a whole number (which in the case of 166.66666666 would be 167). I suggest that if you can set the decimal places on your calculator, you set it for three places after the decimal place. Test writers will usually not provide answers that are so close that rounding could make a difference between selecting the right or wrong answer. But you should be prepared for any possibility, like the following:

Assuming the total value of the property to be $190,000 and the total net income to be $13,680, what would be the capitalization rate?

A. 6.5%
B. 7%
C. 7.2%
D. 7.5%

Here, if your calculator is set to use a floating decimal or automatically rounds off to two decimal places, the answer will come up as 0.07, which you would take to be 7% (Choice B), when the correct answer is actually 0.072, or 7.2% (Choice C).

Gross multipliers

Another way value is calculated uses multipliers to convert income into value.

The gross income multiplier (GIM) is usually based on annual income. The gross rent multiplier (GRM) is based on monthly income. The formulas are the same regardless of which multiplier is used. You only need to make sure you use annual or monthly rent appropriately.

Income × GRM = Value

Value ÷ Income = GRM

Value ÷ GRM = Income

For purposes of these formulas, sales price and value are considered to be the same.

Example 1: A property has a gross monthly income of $3,000. Properties in this area of this type are selling at a GRM of 120. What is the value of the property?

$3,000 × 120 = $360,000

Example 2: A property has an annual income of $35,000. It sold for $700,000. What is its GIM?

$700,000 ÷ $35,000 = 20

Remember: GIMs use annual numbers.

Example 3: A property that is valued at $550,000 sells at a GRM of 110. What is its monthly income?

$550,000 ÷ 110 = $5,000 per month

California Department of Real Estate District Offices

The Department of Real Estate (DRE) has five district offices. Although the phone numbers for the district offices are listed in this appendix, because of the volume of telephone inquiries, you may experience difficulty in getting through to one or more of the offices. If you're seeking general information, try calling a different office than the one closest to you. If you need specific information about your test site, you'll probably need to call your local office. If you're looking to get information on your application, you may need to call the Sacramento office.

Much of the information you need is available on the DRE Web site, including applications and E-licensing—a process that allows you to register and conduct all your business via the Internet. Taking care of business via the Internet may be your best avenue. It's quick and painless, although the DRE Web site can sometimes be a bit difficult to use. Be patient—it's very doable online.

For information on registering for the exam, visit the DRE Web site at www.dre.ca.gov. You can register for the exam online at https://secure.dre.ca.gov/elicensing/ or by mail or fax (instructions for mailing/faxing the application are available at www.dre.ca.gov/salessch.htm).

Fresno
2550 Mariposa Mall, Room 3070
Fresno, CA 93721-2273
Phone: 559-445-5009

Los Angeles
320 W. Fourth St., Suite 350
Los Angeles, CA 90013-1105
Phone: 213-620-2072

Oakland
1515 Clay St., Suite 702
Oakland, CA 94612-1462
Phone: 510-622-2552

Sacramento
2201 Broadway
Sacramento, CA 95818-2500
Phone: 916-227-0900

San Diego
1350 Front St., Suite 3064
San Diego, CA 92101-3687
Phone: 619-525-4192

Testing Centers

Tests are usually administered at the main testing offices, which are in bold in the following sections. You can request to take your test at one of the newer satellite testing centers, but the Department of Real Estate cautions that those testing centers fill up quickly and you may be scheduled at one of the main testing centers if your satellite of choice is booked.

Los Angeles District

CPS Human Resource Services
1380 S. Sanderson Ave., Suite 100
Anaheim, CA 92806

CPS Human Resource Services
1012 E. Cooley Dr., Suite A
Colton, CA 92324

CPS Human Resource Services
100 W. Broadway, Suite 500
Glendale, CA 91210

Department of Real Estate
320 W. Fourth St., Suite 855
Los Angeles, CA 90017

The Pasadena Center
300 E. Green St.
Pasadena, CA 91101

Sheraton Pasadena Hotel
3030 E. Cordova St.
Pasadena, CA 91101

CPS Human Resource Services
124 Carmen Lane, Suite F
Santa Maria, CA 93458

Fresno District

CPS Human Resource Services
1320 E. Shaw Ave., Suite 138
Fresno, CA 93726

State Office Building
2550 Mariposa Mall, Room 1027
Fresno, CA 93721-2273

State Office Building
2550 Mariposa Mall, Room 1036
Fresno, CA 93721-2273

State Office Building
2550 Mariposa Mall, Room 3074
Fresno, CA 93721-2273

Oakland District

CPS Human Resource Services
1814 Franklin St., Suite 400
Oakland, CA 94612

Elihu M. Harris State Office Building
1515 Clay St., Room 703
Oakland, CA 94612-1462

Elihu M. Harris State Office Building
1515 Clay St., Second Floor, Room 1
Oakland, CA 94612-1462

Elihu M. Harris State Office Building
1515 Clay St., Second Floor, Room 2
Oakland, CA 94612-1462

CPS Human Resource Services
200 Wyatt Dr., Suite 11
Santa Clara, CA 95054

Sacramento District

CPS Human Resource Services
1300 Hilltop Dr., Suite 200
Redding, CA 96003

Department of Real Estate
2200 X St., Room 120B
Sacramento, CA 95818-2500

CPS Human Resource Services
825 Riverside Parkway, Suite 100
West Sacramento, CA 95605

San Diego District

CPS Human Resource Services
6160 Mission Gorge Rd., Suite 204
San Diego, CA 92120

Department of Real Estate
1350 Front St., Suite 3064
San Diego, CA 92101-3687

Notes

Notes

Notes

Notes

Notes

Notes

LaVergne, TN USA
12 October 2010

200463LV00001B/34/P

9 780470 036990